The Wines and Wineries of
OREGON'S
Willamette Valley

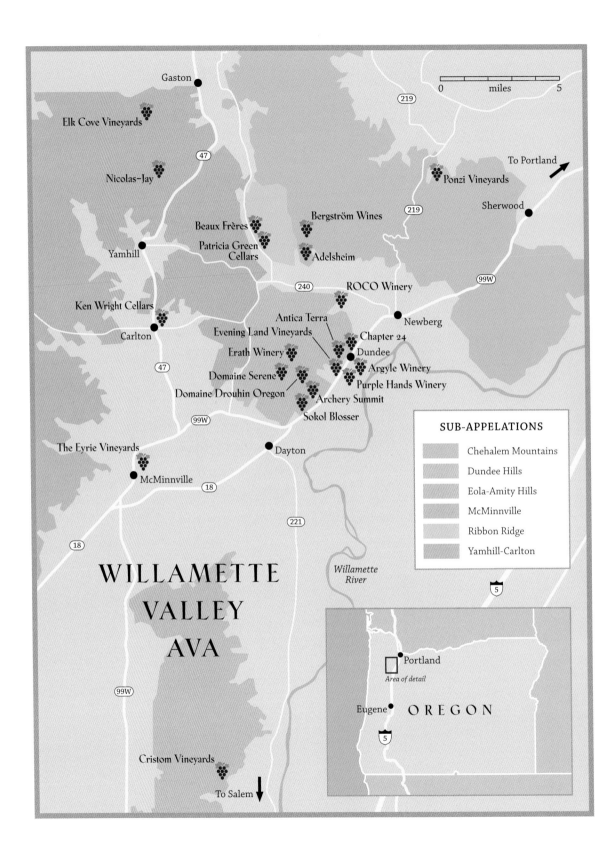

Gaston

Elk Cove Vineyards

Nicolas-Jay

47

219

Ponzi Vineyards

To Portland

Sherwood

219

Beaux Frères

Bergström Wines

Patricia Green
Cellars

Adelsheim

Yamhill

99W

240

ROCO Winery

Ken Wright Cellars

Antica Terra

Newberg

Evening Land Vineyards

Chapter 24

Carlton

Erath Winery

Dundee

47

Domaine Serene

Argyle Winery

Domaine Drouhin Oregon

Purple Hands Winery

Archery Summit

Sokol Blosser

The Eyrie Vineyards

Dayton

McMinnville

18

221

18

SUB-APPELATIONS

Chehalem Mountains

Dundee Hills

Eola-Amity Hills

McMinnville

Ribbon Ridge

Yamhill-Carlton

WILLAMETTE
VALLEY
AVA

Willamette
River

5

99W

Portland

Area of detail

Cristom Vineyards

Eugene

OREGON

To Salem

5

0   miles   5

The Wines and Wineries of
OREGON'S
Willamette Valley

From Pinot Noir to Chardonnay

NICK WISE & LINDA SUNSHINE

Principal Photography by
JULIE WISE

A WELCOME ENTERPRISES BOOK

OVERLOOK OMNIBUS

Contents

Page 3: **Pinot Noir grapes at Elk Cove Vineyards, in Gaston.**

Introduction
Valley of the Grapes

In 2010, after working in the wine business for nearly two decades, Nick noticed a burgeoning trend. Suddenly, it seemed as though celebrities were slapping their names on wine labels and promoting themselves as working winemakers. Nick wondered if these celebrities were actually involved in the winemaking process, and he wanted to learn more. That was the beginning of our first adventure in making books together.

We embarked on an extensive wine tour, a journey that took us from Napa to Tuscany to find the famous people who were claiming to be modern winemakers. After our book, *Celebrity Vineyards*, was published in 2013, we wrote a follow-up edition that focused solely on the West Coast. *California Celebrity Vineyards: From Napa to Los Olivos in Search of Great Wine* was published in February 2016.

By this time, another winemaking region had captured Nick's imagination and his palate: The Pacific Northwest. He'd discovered that his favorite wine shop, Handford's, in West London, near where he lives, had begun stocking wines from places called Cristom, Domaine Serene, and Archery Summit. With this introduction to the wines of Oregon, Nick realized that these Pinot Noirs could easily compete with some of his favorites from Burgundy. This was both a delight and a surprise. Nick wanted to visit the region, one of the few winemaking areas of the world he had never seen.

The original idea was to write a book about the wines of Oregon and Washington called *The Wines of the Pacific Northwest*. To that end, we packed up and headed off to Portland in March 2016. Joining us was Nick's recent bride, Julie, who would be our resident photographer.

We started where most of Nick's favorite wineries were located—in the Willamette Valley, which runs southward from the Columbia River at Portland for nearly 150 miles. The region is divided into six sub-AVAs: Dundee Hills, Eola-Amity Hills, Ribbon Ridge, McMinnville, Yamhill-Carlton District, and Chehalem Mountains.

Pages 6–7 and opposite: **Views of the gorgeous vineyards at Domaine Serene, in Dayton.**
Above: **Our first rental, in Gaston, designed by famed winemaker Tony Soter.**

Our first trip to the valley was nothing short of amazing. We gathered a wealth of material—the people we met were incredibly knowledgeable and passionate about winemaking. And the wines were first class. Though we began with labels Nick knew, we soon expanded our base to wineries that were not distributed in London. One winemaker would suggest another, and every day we encountered a new amazing vintage. Of course, we hit a few clinkers along the way, but overall, the good (and the great) far outweighed the mediocre.

Wine lovers around the world know that this is what a regional wine-tasting tour is all about: the thrill of discovery.

McMinnville Madness

We came home to Los Angeles after several weeks to realize we'd barely scratched the surface of the Willamette Valley. We wanted to go back and find the winemakers who were not available to meet with us during that first tour, learn more about the wineries we loved, and research the many others that had been recommended. We decided to forget about Washington (and the rest of Oregon), at least for the moment. Instead, we would concentrate on this one particular region—the Willamette Valley.

We returned to Portland in May 2016, and, now more familiar with the area, rented a house in McMinnville, in the heart of the valley. Walking through this quaint and historic town, we noticed

that people in the streets were dressed, well, a bit oddly, to say the least. Folks were wandering around downtown wearing aluminum antennas that reflected the sunlight as they bobbed and swayed. Others wore entire outfits constructed of foil or costumes straight out of an outer space B-movie.

We soon discovered we had arrived during the annual UFO Festival, a traditional McMinnville event attended by thousands. Founded in 1999 to honor what are considered to be the first photos of a UFO sighting, snapped in 1950 by local farmers Evelyn and Paul Trent (images are viewable online), the festival has turned into an epic celebration of all things extraterrestrial. "As a result," said Cathy Martin, Argyle Winery's marketing coordinator, "there was no aluminum foil to be found in all of McMinnville" the weekend of the event.

Most of the Oregonians we met take the festival with a shrug and an indulgent smile, but at dinner one night, Nick met a woman who swore there were "at least eight aliens" she

A streetlamp is decorated for the UFO Festival, in McMinnville.

Pinot Noir grapes.

knew personally who lived in town. We soon discovered that Oregon is the kind of place that indulges and even supports people with all kinds of passions. It is one of the reasons we fell in love with it.

Of course, the main passion we discovered was for Pinot Noir. There are only a handful of places on the planet where this finicky grape can grow, and thanks to many factors such as climate and soil, the Willamette Valley is one of them. Though it may be obvious today that this land is perfectly suited to cultivating Pinot Noir, that was not always the case. In fact, the wine industry in Oregon is only 50 years old. Compare that to some of the vineyards in Burgundy that date back to the 15th century, and you begin to understand just how young this winemaking community is.

In time, we learned that a group of extraordinarily daring and prescient people risked everything to settle here and take on the challenge of establishing a brand-new industry.

How We Picked Our Wineries

By some accounts, there are now close to 600 wineries in the Willamette Valley, whereas in the early 1970s, there were only a dozen. Since we could not begin to cover even a fraction of the current wineries, our idea was to focus specifically on wineries that either had significant historical importance to the valley and the industry or were symbolic of the smaller, cult wineries that embody the spirit of innovation and experimentation that defines Oregon wines. We wanted to explore each winery in some depth to present an overall view of what it takes to build a winery from scratch (both in the early days and today) and—from the perspective of the second-generation winemakers—what it's like to carry forth the legacy of the original pioneers.

Nick Wise tasting Purple Hands wines at our rental house, in McMinnville.

A Hunch and a Prayer

The story of Oregon Pinot Noir goes back to the late 1960s and early 1970s. Up until then, the main cash crops in the area were filberts (also known as hazelnuts), cherries, plums, and other produce—almost everything *but* grapes. It was thought, at the time, that California was the only place a vineyard would thrive on the West Coast; but some adventurous souls disagreed.

Richard Sommer is generally credited as the first to plant a vineyard in Roseburg (now the Umpqua Valley AVA), in 1961, releasing his first vintage in 1967. Sommer, a UC Davis graduate, encouraged the other early winemakers who followed: Charles Coury and David Lett.

While at UC Davis in 1962, Charles Coury had written a master thesis titled, "Cold Climate Amelioration Hypothesis," in which he hypothesized that vinifera varietals produce their best-quality wines when ripened just at the limit of their growing season. He chose Oregon to prove his theory. Coury, whose early contributions were seminal to the growth of the industry, was also one of the first in the States to be interested in Pinot Noir clones. In 1965, he purchased an abandoned 45-acre farm near Forest Grove and planted Pinot Noir. According to those who were around back then, his early wines were spectacular. Coury was influential in other ways: his ideas inspired many of Oregon's labeling regulations, quarantines on plant material, and the establishment of a research center at Oregon State University. In the 1980s, Coury returned to California to work in the microbrewery industry; his historic property was sold and today is the David Hill Winery. Coury passed away in 2004, at the age of 73, and his contributions to the industry have largely been forgotten, perhaps because he left Oregon before the world discovered its potential for Pinot.

Early days at Adelsheim, in Newberg, circa 1980, during harvest.

Much more well known and celebrated is David Lett, who came to Oregon shortly after Coury. In 1965, Lett trucked 3,000 cuttings from the lab at UC Davis to the hills of Corvallis and named his vineyard Eyrie. His 1970 release was a few hundred cases of what he called "Oregon Spring Wine." Though the beginnings were inauspicious, Lett's wines improved markedly every year and became the standard-bearer in the area. For his accomplishments, his very high criteria for excellence, his stubborn pursuit of the best his vineyard could offer, and his Hemingway-style beard, he was dubbed "Papa Pinot" by his fellow winemakers. Today, his legacy continues thanks to his son Jason, a second-generation winemaker, who took over the winery after his father died in 2008.

Not long after Coury and Lett came to the Willamette Valley, other winemakers began migrating from California, attracted by the climate, the soil, and the availability of inexpensive land. These families included the Eraths, the Ponzis, the Sokol Blossers, the Adelsheims, and the Campbells, among others. It can't be overemphasized that when they made the move north, they had no idea if grapes would prosper here. They risked everything on a hunch and a prayer.

Working Together

When they first arrived in Oregon, driving up in their VW buses and flatbed trucks, these early winemakers sought the best plots of land on which to experiment with various clones. They were learning how to grow grapes, make wine, and establish a new industry. None of them, they told us, came here primarily to make money. Mostly, they wanted to find a way to live on the land, work in collaboration with like-minded people, and raise their families in joyful celebration. They also wanted to help the State of Oregon, which everyone believed was akin to a paradise on Earth. They worked hard to be supportive of one another and share what they were learning in the fields and the fermenters. They understood that working together would benefit everyone.

Information was freely traded among friends at dinners and parties as well as at organized conferences, monthly meetings, and other social gatherings. It's hard to imagine anything like this happening in the more competitive winemaking regions of the world, such as Napa or Burgundy. David Adelsheim, who came here with his family in the early seventies, says, "Without the collaboration of the wine growers, our vineyard would not be where it is today. The ten families who made wine before 1980 ultimately crafted something that worked. None of us could have done this alone."

Luisa Ponzi, a second-generation winemaker who grew up on the vineyard created by her parents, Dick and

Above: **Bud break at Domaine Serene.**
Pages 14–15: **Aerial view of Cristom's Eileen Vineyard, in Salem.**

A Pinot Noir harvest at Ponzi Vineyards, in Sherwood.

Nancy Ponzi, remembers the assistance and advice her father received from "… some really great and helpful grape-growing neighbors at Erath, Eyrie, Elk Cove, and Adelsheim." And that culture of collaboration is still thriving in the valley today. "By sharing what would and wouldn't work with others, we don't have to repeat the same mistakes over and over," Gary Horner, the Erath winemaker, points out. Chris Mazepink, the current winemaker and GM at Archery Summit, agrees. "If my press breaks during the harvest, I can call Véronique Drouhin [of Domaine Drouhin Oregon] and she will say, 'Come on up, you can press your grapes here.' It's not like that in places like Napa," says Chris.

Like Falling in Love

In 1969, Dick Erath planted 26 varieties of grapes, in order to determine which grapes would prosper in the soil of Oregon. Surprisingly, his most successful varieties included Pinot Noir, Pinot Gris, and Pinot Blanc. The result of Erath's experiment would prove vital to the burgeoning industry as he and the other early winemakers began to figure out what grapes could be harvested here and, just as important, which ones were not worth the time and effort.

Ultimately they discovered that the Pinot Noir grape, albeit super-finicky, thrives in this climate, though not without challenges—it ripens quickly and is very sensitive to its environment. "Pinot Noir is such a delicate princess of a grape, it knows everything you've done to it and it remembers," says Grace Evenstad of Domaine Serene.

So, what entices winemakers to pursue this difficult grape? Often we heard about an "aha" moment (or what Jason Lett calls the "road to Damascus" moment) that set a winemaker on the trail of Pinot Noir. We discovered that a particular bottle, tasted at just the right moment, could alter the course of a career. We like to compare it to falling in love—the first time is truly unforgettable.

"For me it was a 1954 Grand Cru Burgundy," Gary Horner tells us, with a smile on his face. "I took it to my nose—it was loaded with violets, flower aromas and tea. The wine was still alive. That was my magical 'aha' moment." Not long after, Horner quit his high-paying career as a pharmacist, moved to Oregon, and took a job on the bottling line at Bethel Heights for $6 an hour. It was the start of his education in viticulture.

An exceptional Pinot Noir was the inspiration for Paul Gerrie, the founder of Cristom, and he can still recall the moment he took his first sip. "It was a 1980 Echezeaux, and it was astonishing," reports Gerrie. "From that point on, I was hooked on Pinot!" For Dick Erath, it was love at first sip with a 1955 Inglenook Pinot Noir.

Over and over, we'd hear a version of this story: a brilliant bottle of Pinot Noir giving rise to a new appreciation of wine and, ultimately, a career in winemaking.

French Soul, Oregon Soil

The Willamette Valley has never stopped evolving. Since the arrival of Richard Sommer, Charles Coury, David Lett, and the families who followed, there has been a continual influx of innovative winemakers from every winemaking region in the world, who are experimenting with, expanding, and altering the landscape of Oregon. A second wave landed in the 1980s. Rollin Soles came to Dundee to start Argyle and create a

The tasting room at Domaine Serene after a winter snowstorm.

An old truck at Beaux Frères, in Newberg.

sparkling-wine empire. Ken Wright appeared around the same time to explore different methods of farming that would enhance the soil and focus on site-specific Pinots. Robert "Gary" Andrus came a few years later to blast open a mountainside, unearthing an underground cave for his barrel and tasting room. He then shocked everyone by retailing his wine at the unprecedented price of $50 a bottle, an affirmation that the wines of Oregon were worthy of such respect.

And then there was the French invasion, triggered by the arrival of the Drouhin family, whose winemaking pedigree dates back at least a century. They arrived in 1986, bringing to their vineyards a wealth of knowledge, from hard-earned experience, that they shared with their fellow winemakers, profoundly altering the course of winemaking in the valley.

The French connection continued in 2005, when Evening Land's Mark Tarlov purchased the extraordinary Seven Springs Vineyard in the Eola-Amity Hills and hired Dominique Lafon, from the famed Domaine des Comtes Lafon in Burgundy, as his consulting winemaker.

After leaving Evening Land, Tarlov created his second winery, the innovative Chapter 24. Both these ventures aimed for Burgundian perfection and were created in conjunction with a legendary French producer. For Chapter 24, Tarlov joined forces with Viscount Louis-Michel Ligier-Belair, whose vineyard, Domaine des Comtes Ligier-Belair, in Vosne-Romanée, dates to 1815, when Napoleon granted the land to his family.

And, recently, other French vintners such as Jacques Lardière at Maison Louis Jadot and Jean-Nicolas Méo of Burgundy's Domaine Méo-Camuzet and Oregon's Nicolas-Jay have arrived to make their mark in the valley.

Land in the Valley

Today, no winemaker would consider buying uncultivated land without testing the soil and doing extensive geological surveys, but in the early years, the process was a lot simpler. "In the late sixties,

Opposite: **Sunset at Adelsheim's Bryan Creek Vineyard.**

The garden at Cristom Vineyards.

early seventies, if anybody claimed to know anything about the soil or the climates at a site, they would've been considered delusionary," says David Adelsheim with a laugh.

Exploring the various terroirs in the Willamette Valley was certainly an eye-opening experience for young winemakers back in the day. One of the things that most interests us about Oregon is that, even now, there is so much land available for planting. "It would be naïve to think we've tapped into everything Oregon has to offer," cautions Chris Mazepink. "Only 2 percent of the state's acreage has been turned into wine grapes."

Chardonnay grapes.

Land here also costs a fraction of the price of prime California acreage. Top sites in Napa sell from $400,000 to $500,000 an acre and $150,000 an acre on the Central Coast. In Oregon, the cost drops to about $35,000 an acre, according to a *New York Times* article by Paul Sullivan (September 2016).

The Future is Chardonnay

When we asked about the future of the Willamette Valley, Rollin Soles of ROCO had only one word, "Chardonnay!" This was an oft-repeated sentiment by the winemakers we interviewed. Of course, no one can predict with certainty whether Chardonnay will become as synonymous with the valley as Pinot Noir, but everyone acknowledges that Oregon winemaking has come a long way and that there are major changes looming on the horizon. What began as a bold move by a dozen visionary families has evolved into a thriving and sustainable wine industry. Today, Oregon wines are sold in every state and many foreign countries.

It's an exciting time to be making wine in the Willamette Valley (although we suspect it was *always* exciting here). Winemakers who come to this valley are free to explore new ideas and move the bar of excellence ever higher. Almost every winemaker we met wants to experiment with a new grape or create a different vintage in the hopes of bringing something unique to the industry. Jason Lett wants to work with the Trousseau grape from the Jura region of Eastern France. Grace and Ken Evenstad, at Domaine Serene, have started producing Coeur Blanc—made from just the core of white Pinot Noir grapes (no skin contact)— which has never before been done in the States. Cody Wright, at Purple Hands, would love to grow Nebbiolo; and Rollin Soles is releasing his first vintage of ROCO sparkling wine.

In the tradition of Oregon's collaborative spirit, the winemakers we met were extremely generous with their time, their wine, and their passion for the Willamette Valley. Steve Doerner took us on a phenomenal three-hour barrel tasting in the Cristom cellars. Patricia Green gave us a walking tour of her gorgeous vineyards that left us panting and exhilarated. Nate Klostermann at Argyle indulged our love of sparkling wine with special treats from the library and then hung out with us as we polished off all his delicious offerings. Cody Wright insisted we take home an entire complimentary case of his brilliant wine, which was a tremendous gift.

Above: **Beaux Frères's Pork Chop and author Linda Sunshine's Bernie get acquainted.**
Pages 22–23: **Ponzi's Aurora Vineyard glows in the morning light and mist.**

As for us, we will certainly be returning to visit our new friends and explore some of the wineries we missed the first time around. Though we know we ought to focus next on Washington State, the Willamette Valley is calling us back. You could say that, like so many others, we left our hearts and our palates in the verdant hills of Oregon.

Nick Wise & Linda Sunshine

The Eyrie Vineyards

ORIGINAL VINES

Pinot noir

2012

Chapter 1
Papa Pinot

THE EYRIE VINEYARDS

McMinnville

"Barrel tasting," says Jason Lett, "is like open-ing the door to a teenager's room without knocking—you never know what you are going to get." With that, Jason scrambles up some very rickety wooden scaffolding, Spider-Man style, to draw us a tasting from one of his uppermost barrels. That's when we know we are in for a fun ride at Eyrie.

Located in the heart of McMinnville, a town in the Willamette Valley we've come to love, the winery where Eyrie is bottled and stored was converted from a former abattoir. "Turkeys were one of the big agricultural crops here in Oregon in the 1950s," Jason tells us, "and this is one of the spaces where they met their end." Nick wants to know if they were wild turkeys and Jason laughs. "No, they were far from wild. They were white, domesticated 'breasts on legs.'"

Jason's parents, David and Diana Lett, rented the former slaughterhouse in 1970 for $20 a month, then purchased and converted the building. It has remained the home of Eyrie ever since. "In the late 1960s, my folks had a nice design to create a little gravity-flow win-ery but no bank would lend them the money to build it," explains Jason. "They were told there

Opposite: **Eyrie label artwork by Jason Lett.**
Above: **Diana and David Lett, 1967.**

was no future for grapes in Oregon and that they should grow walnuts, or even turkeys."

But David Lett had other ideas about the Willamette Valley and he was not about to be dissuaded by a bunch of bankers.

From Root Canals to Rootstocks

Born in 1939 in Salt Lake City, David Lett was on his way to dental school in San Francisco when he took a detour through Northern California's Wine Country. Driving past

25

Souverain on Howell Mountain in Napa Valley, he saw someone cleaning barrels and thought it looked interesting. He stopped the car and walked over to meet winemaker Lee Stewart. "Dad rolls barrels around for an afternoon and then calls his folks and tells them he's not going to dental school, he's going to work for Lee Stewart," Jason explains. "The only way he saved himself from being disowned was by telling his parents he would go to UC and get a degree in grape growing."

Good to his word, Lett graduated UC in two years with a degree in viticulture. "Dad had fallen in love with Pinot Noir. His professors at the time were starting to emphasize to their students that they needed to find the right climate to grow grapes and told them to look outside California for Pinot Noir," says Jason. "So Dad went to Europe in 1964 and traveled through France, Portugal, Spain, Germany, and Switzerland, talking to growers."

The trip provided Lett with the kind of experience and on-the-ground training that would be hard to duplicate today. Armed with letters of introduction from the chair of UC's viticulture school, he was granted access to legendary cellars. One night he would sleep in the back of his station wagon, and the next he'd be welcomed into a chateau. It was like gaining a master's degree in viticulture without paying tuition. "He would go around asking why they did things a certain way and they would invariably tell him it was tradition. He learned that people in Bordeaux didn't grow Pinot Noir because it ripens too quickly in their climate," says Jason. The trip cemented

David Lett with his original cuttings, 1965.

Lett's commitment to grow Pinot Noir in an environment analogous to Burgundy's. He went back to UC Davis and studied the work of Victor Pulliat, a French physician and agronomist from the late 1800s who believed that wine grapes should be matched to climate. Lett looked at soil records and weather charts and started homing in on the Willamette Valley. "I wanted to make the great American Pinot Noir," David Lett once told an interviewer. "And I figured there was no climate cool enough in California to do that." His professors at UC Davis, especially Harold "Hod" Berg, encouraged him in his quest. And so, in 1965, David Lett arrived in Oregon, sight unseen, with 3,000 cuttings in his truck.

The cuttings were from the research vineyards at UC Davis, as Lett didn't want to plant anything imported from Europe that might contain viruses or wood disease. He was committed to starting a clean, new industry and wine-growing region; the only question was where to begin. (There were no AVAs in Oregon at that time; the first wasn't designated until 1974.) Though Lett had identified the Willamette Valley, he didn't know precisely where to plant his cuttings. As it turned out, his instincts for picking places to put his grapes would prove to be prescient. Eventually, he chose a grassy field outside of Corvallis with deep alluvial soils. "This was the worst place possible for mature grapes," says Jason, "but the very best place if you're trying to build roots on young plants. So Dad planted the vines and started looking for the right site to move them [once they matured]."

To support himself, Lett worked for a textbook company, and while driving around making sales calls, he kept a soil auger in the trunk of his car to scout possible properties. At a business conference he met and—six weeks later—married Diana, who also worked for the publisher. Their honeymoon was spent planting cuttings. About her young life in Oregon, Diana once said, "Three months after meeting David Lett in 1966, I was Diana Lett, standing out in the middle of a field of grapevines in Oregon, with a shovel and a brand-new yellow rainsuit. I didn't have a clue what I was doing, but I was thrilled to be in on the opening chapter of a great adventure." Then she adds with a laugh, "In the 1960s, being a winemaker was about as valid an occupation as being a shepherd."

After a year and a half, Lett honed in on the red hills of Dundee as the ideal location for a vineyard because of the consistency of the soils. "The Jory soils are what led Dad here, but honestly, if he'd had the opportunity to make wine anywhere else in the world, he would probably have picked Portugal, which he loved," says Jason.

Still, David Lett had great faith in Oregon and staked his life's ambitions on the cuttings that he planted. In his journal from 1965, he wrote, "So many hopes and dreams are held in these fragile leaves and tender shoots which seemed a few months ago to be only dead sticks pushed into Oregon mud. I cannot help but feel now that success will be ours."

The land the Letts eventually purchased was an abandoned prune orchard with a pair of red-tailed hawks nesting in a nearby fir tree. A feeling of kinship with the hawks inspired Diana to name the vineyard Eyrie, a 15th-century medieval word meaning "hawk's nest."

The shallow volcanic soil at the Eyrie Vineyards.

Eyrie Vineyards.

From the beginning, Lett's philosophy was to interfere as little as possible with the processes of nature. Though "sustainability" was not a buzzword in the 1970s, Lett farmed as organically as possible, without the use of insecticides, herbicides, or systemic fungicides. The vines were grown on their own roots and without irrigation. He believed healthier vines made better wines, but he also wanted to keep the land itself healthy and safe for future generations.

A Beautiful Mystery

From the very start, David Lett had a different mind-set from the rest of the pioneering winemakers in the valley. While everyone was a novice in this great experiment to make Pinot Noir in Oregon, other winemakers focused on producing a "California-style" wine—very extracted, dark, and almost Syrah-like. Conversely, Lett decided to make a much more delicate, expressive, and lighter wine—more like the Burgundy Pinot Noir he preferred to drink himself. As a true artist, he had a vision and followed his own instincts. If a vintage didn't meet his standards, he wouldn't release it. Lett was so disappointed with his first 1970 vintage that he refused to call it Pinot Noir, instead marketing it as "Oregon Spring Wine," for $2.75 a bottle with a label that informed consumers this was a "... wine to be served on all informal occasions." Lett also wanted to stockpile vintages so that he could taste how they aged over time. In fact, selling the wine never seemed to be a top priority, and because of this, Lett began building what would become an unprecedented and huge library of unreleased wines.

Lett's wines were never the flashiest, partly because his style aimed for delicacy and longevity even though the trend, particularly in Oregon, was for immediate pleasure and super ripeness. The famous wine critic Robert Parker Jr. developed a dislike of the wines and the man himself, but the bullish David Lett didn't seem to care. Despite the criticism, he continued to make wines that were to his own liking, and was unaffected by public opinion or popular trends.

As a newly created venture in a very ancient industry, the wines of Oregon were relatively unknown until the late 1970s when, in 1979,

Eyrie Vineyard's 1975 South Block Reserve Pinot Noir placed in the top 10 at the Gault Millau Wine Olympics in Paris, beating many French competitors. After a rematch was requested by noted Burgundian producer Robert Drouhin, a second contest was held in Beaune the following year and this time Eyrie garnered second place. "I was dancing in the driveway," David declared at the time about this benchmark achievement that helped launch the entire wine industry in Oregon. (Robert Drouhin and his daughter Véronique were so impressed with the Oregon wine that in 1987, they purchased land in Dundee Hills, not far from the original Eyrie vineyard, and established Domaine Drouhin Oregon.)

Eyrie wines began slowly but steadily building a substantial following, especially in Europe, and this raised their profile considerably. Wine lovers began to appreciate that Eyrie wines were special and unique. On release, they were delicate, unexpressive with high acidity, and seemingly low on fruit and tannin, but then, with even short-term cellar age, they made a complete U-turn and transformed into a complex wine with great depth of flavor. Many of the world's best wines can hold with age, but very few improve like Eyrie's. It's a mystery, even to the winemaker, but as Nick likes to say, "it's a beautiful mystery."

Like Father, Like Son

Jason Lett started working in the vineyard when he was three years old. To train his palate, his father would play a game with him and

Above: **Jason Lett.**
Pages 30–31: **The Eyrie Vineyards in fall.**

his siblings. "He would buy a roll of Life Savers," Jason said on a radio show not long ago. "He would hold a Life Saver in his hand and we would have to smell it. If we could tell him what flavor it was, he would give it to us. But if we couldn't, he would eat it."

As a kid, Jason enjoyed working on the farm for pocket change, but during his teenage years, he found it far less interesting. So, as a young adult, he left home and traveled around

the United States, particularly through places like Colorado and New Mexico. The skills he'd picked up on the family farm served him well and he easily found work at biological field stations and wildlife refuges. He met his wife, an archaeologist, on a dig and started following her all over the country. Eventually, he went back to college, and got a degree in botany in the late 1990s.

His parents were not entirely happy when, in his late twenties, he decided to return to Oregon to work at Eyrie. "My mother often hinted that I should go to law school, sort of like my dad's parents did with him and dental school," Jason says. "When I told them I wanted to come back into the family business, they seemed kind of disappointed at first." When he did return to the Willamette Valley,

he found it difficult to work with his father. "It was like having two cooks trying to stir the same pot in a very small kitchen. It wasn't working for either of us. I was looking around and seeing things that could be changed for the better. And, of course, Dad had developed these techniques over years of trial and error and he was not going to change just because some young kid was telling him to do so. We always kept a good, loving father-son relationship, but the family business was something else. Those are two hard things that should not be put together," explains Jason, who started making his own wine, Black Cap, while managing other vineyards in the Willamette Valley.

Then, in about 2005, David Lett got sick, and it was clear that his health was failing. "He really started to get serious about what was going to happen to the winery," says Jason. The prodigal son returned home. A few years later, in 2008, David Lett died, having been nicknamed "Papa Pinot" for both his pioneering efforts in Oregon and for the silver beard and irascible style that many likened to Hemingway. Jason assumed stewardship of Eyrie Vineyards.

Since then, Jason has kept his father's initial vision and style: not pandering toward making bigger, richer, and more modernly styled wines that are currently trendy. "Dad decided to go his own route even though it was kind of unpopular at the time. He just worked through it, making the kind of wines he wanted to make," says Jason, who compares winemaking to the fickle world of fashion. "Hemlines go up

Jason Lett in the Eyrie Vineyards' office.

Early vintages from the Eyrie Vineyards, including its first from 1970, "Oregon Spring Wine."

and hemlines go down. Similarly, grapes come into fashion and then fall away. In the 1970s, everyone planted Riesling because Blue Nun was in fashion. Ultimately, it was overcropped, and when people got bored with it, the farmers tore out the grapes."

While the style of Eyrie has remained constant amid the chaos of changing tastes, Jason eagerly embraces new techniques such as whole-cluster fermentation. His interest in the minutiae of oak's influence on wine illustrates his desire not to stand still but to improve his wines. He has also managed to change the look of the bottles, creating his own illustrations for the labels. He is carrying on both the taste profile and the individualistic artistic vision initiated by his father.

Today Eyrie produces about 9,000 cases of some of the best Oregon wines being made in the Willamette Valley. And they are still

making wine in the former abattoir, though part of Jason's three-point plan for the future is to change that.

The Plan

The first part of Jason's vision for Eyrie involves the 6,000 cases of wine that comprise the extensive library compiled by his father. From his very first vintage, in 1970, David Lett seemed almost reluctant to sell the wines he was making, and over the years, he became something of a hoarder. It is highly unusual for a winery the size of Eyrie to have such a vast library of vintage wines; but it is a lucky situation for the consumer.

Maintaining such a collection of wines is very complicated: storage is difficult and expensive and not all bottles age the same way. In 2008, Jason held a tasting of library wines and discovered that not every bottle had withstood the test of time. This was unacceptable to him. "Each bottle ages differently and is like its own little snowflake," says Jason. "So the first thing is to figure out consistency. I want to be able to release the wines but I don't want people to be disappointed with a flawed bottle of Oregon wine."

To this end, Jason has created a "Cellar Certification" program to ensure the highest quality of every bottle in the library. Each bottle is opened and assessed. Corked and overly oxidized wines are discarded. On average, about 40 percent of every vintage doesn't make the cut.

Custom-designed equipment is used to empty the worthy bottles into a drum, where they are blended for consistency. The original bottles are washed and dried three times and flushed with nitrogen. Then the wine is bottled, recorked, sealed, and released as a "Cellar Certified" library wine.

Jason has also devised a formula for pricing these bottles. "We take the current vintage price and then, depending on what kind of wine it is, we add a fee for each year it has been stored and for the certification process. We add $5 a year for a South Block Pinot Noir and $2 a year for Pinot Gris, for example."

It took Jason about five years to work out this process for certification. "We've got it dialed in now," he says, "and we're releasing about seven library wines per year from different vintages."

It's a time-consuming and expensive process, but one that Jason feels is essential. Unlike his father, Jason does not plan to hold on to large quantities of wines to be sold in the future.

The library wines that deviate even slightly from Jason's high standards become part of a multi-vintage blend in a process called Solera. (*Solera* is a Spanish word that means "on the ground" and refers to the lower level of a set of barrels.) Solera is a method of fractional blending, where wines from different vintages are transferred from barrel to barrel, top to bottom, with the oldest mixtures being on the bottom of the barrel. Thus, the finished product is a mixture of wines from different years. The purpose of this very labor-intensive procedure is to maintain a reliable style and quality. Used in Portugal and Spain, the process usually results in a medium-sweet Port-like wine.

In his mixture, Jason has added about 40 vintages ranging from 1972 to 2015, in the hope that the resultant wine, which ends up being about 17 percent alcohol and is called Equation, will combine attributes of the older vintages with the more recent ones.

The second part of Jason's agenda for the future involves replanting the vineyards. This is due to problems with phylloxera, an aphid that attacks and kills own-rooted vines (vines that are not grafted onto the rootstock). "We're all own-rooted at this point," he tells us, "and that needs to change, or we won't be around for another generation."

Posts and pillars were installed in the 50-year-old winery to hold up the sagging roof.

Jason Lett draws a tasting from a barrel.

Finally, Jason's third goal is to build a new winery. The former abattoir has more than served its purpose in the 50 years since his parents first leased the building. But, as Jason explains, "you can't put 90 percent humidity inside a wooden building for half a century and expect it to remain standing. In the barrel room, for example, we have posts and pillars that are literally propping up the ceiling."

The current structure also has other constraints that have informed the way Eyrie makes wine. "This building is chockablock with limitations," he explains, "that have forced us to do things we probably wouldn't do otherwise. We can't drive a forklift into the building, so everything here is done by hand."

Designing a new winery from the bottom up is an exciting prospect, though having too many choices has its drawbacks. "Some of the best poems I've written were sonnets," says Jason, "and some of the worst were written in free verse. Having limitations is sometimes a good thing."

As an artist, poet, winemaker, and farmer, Jason Lett has many skills to draw upon as he envisions his new winery and the future of Eyrie.

Princess or Monster

Jason's latest venture in the vineyard is planting a varietal called Trousseau Noir, from the Jura region of southeast France. He is the first to try this grape in Oregon and he decided to do it much in the tradition of his father. "My dad planted Pinot Noir because the climate creates opportunity," says Jason. "You can impose style in the winery, but if you're not getting style from the vineyard, then you're not growing it in the right region."

People are always fascinated by what is new and different in the marketplace, but places like Eyrie will always be the gold standard against which new wines are measured. Nick is a dedicated fan of Eyrie wines and is interested in their seamless integration of fruit, acidity, and tannin. He marvels at how they always seem to taste great on release, while other wines need five or six years to mature. Jason nods in agreement when Nick tells him this.

"Dad always used to say that surly teenagers don't always grow up into good adults," Jason says with a smile. "He always liked wines that were pretty right from the beginning. It's a little silly, but he also used to say Pinot Noir can be a princess or a monster, so which would you rather have dinner with?"

2014 Pinot Gris "Original Vines," Dundee Hills

The Pinot Gris 2014 offers up medium gold color and an intriguing bouquet, revealing aromas of smoke, black licorice, black ebony, white pepper, chamomile, melons, ginger, stone fruits, and floral notes matched to superb minerality. It's dry and fresh, yet lush with good full weight and without the usual oiliness one can find in this varietal. A silky palate reveals flavors of stone fruits, spice, and floral and savory elements such as jasmine, nuts, and white pepper. An excellent balance between the white, juicy fruit flavors and acidity carries this nicely subtle yet complex wine to a long, clean mineral finish. A 1994 Pinot Gris tasted side by side was still in perfect condition, showing a more nutty character and fuller body, but was delicious and totally belied its age.

2015 Outcrop Vineyard Pinot Noir, Dundee Hills

The aging capabilities of Eyrie wines are legendary and bewildering despite their almost gentle construct. With an extra 5 to 8 years extended bottle age these wines begin to flesh out, gaining weight and serious complexity; they can last 20 years or more in bottle, not just holding their own but also improving. The delicious Dundee Estate Pinot Noir is delicate and elegant in style, offering bright flavors of cherries, raspberries, cassis, and light oak. The wine is a light crimson color and sits firmly in the red fruit "Beaune-like" camp, expressing mostly higher-toned red fruits with a splash of cassis. It's a firm wine with good structure provided by the steely yet ripe small-grained tannins and high, bright acidity. Grown at an elevation of 350 to 450 feet, this cuvée has lush lower-altitude fruitiness and sweetness, making it more accessible than the other single-vineyard offerings. Light oak and low alcohol levels make the whole portfolio of Eyrie wines seem deceptively drinkable in their youth—yet patience will reward those who wait.

2015 Roland Green Vineyard Pinot Noir, Dundee Hills

Produced at a higher elevation (600 to 700 feet) this high-toned Pinot Noir reveals a sturdier, richer black fruit profile when paired against the Outcrop. More masculine in style, it also reveals greater complexity with a stronger tannic profile but surprisingly lower acidity. The wine is silky and smooth with a nice blend of bright red cherry and raspberry fruits, and floral notes with a dark overlay of black cherry and plums. Nuances of mossy *sous-bois* (forest floor), minerals, cassis, and orange peel make this seductive wine glide over the palate, providing a long, refreshing, and vibrant red fruit and floral flourish on the back end.

2015 Daphne Vineyard Pinot Noir, Dundee Hills

Sourced from a 1.5-acre plot of fruit growing around Jason's house, this wine is hugely enjoyable. Piercing red fruits burst on the nose and palate. Made exclusively from the Burgundian "Pommard" clone of Pinot Noir, these zippy, bright, high-toned flavors of fresh small *framboises*, raspberry, and cherry fruits seem to leap across the palate, accompanied by other nuances such as spearmint, eucalyptus, and very light vanilla, adding complexity. Nice viscosity and texture, matched to high levels of acidity and firm tannins, frame this medium-bodied though quite expressive wine.

1990 Pinot Noir Estate & 1985 Pinot Noir Reserve

The 1990 is a stunning wine. Here is a perfect example of the tremendous and bizarre aging capabilities of the Pinot Noirs made at Eyrie. A light rusty crimson color is followed by a phenomenal bouquet exuding powerful, classic secondary tertiary notes that Pinot wines achieve with extended bottle age. Herbal and malty, with savory notes that bounce around light, delicate flavors of red and black fruits, the wine carries an inherent high acidity but has gained good weight and is generous in sweet fruits for its age. One could sit and enjoy the complexities of this Pinot Noir on the nose and palate for many hours. Tannins are perfectly integrated, and this is drinking wonderfully now. In comparison, the 1985 is more backward and structured in style, exhibiting a darker, browner color and a higher tannin profile. It has gained some of the same lovely secondary characteristics as the 1990 but the fruit is more primary. Both vintages have produced lovely wines.

1992 Chardonnay, Dundee Hills

This delicious wine, the highlight of our tasting with Jason, is another testament to Eyrie wines' shocking longevity. It is not clear how many of the world's other mid-priced chardonnays would have lasted this long, much less gained such serious complexity. This wine, made in the warmest vintage in Oregon's short history, is savory and nutty, with light saddlelike notes and hints of banana, flowers, and honeycomb that cover the lemon-custard flavors. High acidity combined with a sweet ripeness lifts this broad wine to a long, lingering finish.

THE EYRIE VINEYARDS
935 NE 10th Avenue
McMinnville, Oregon 97128
503.472.6315
www.eyrievineyards.com

Tasting Room: open Wednesday through Saturday from 12pm to 5pm, or by appointment

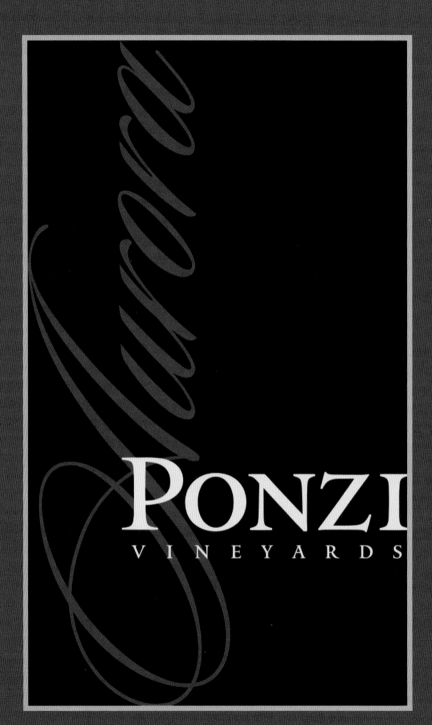

Chapter 2
Hillside of Our Dreams

PONZI VINEYARDS

Sherwood

Ponzi's stunning, contemporary building looks more like a museum than a winery.

Like our friend Jason Lett at Eyrie, Luisa Ponzi is a second-generation winemaker who grew up in her parents' vineyard. However, where Jason is continuing to create and promote his father's cult wines, Luisa, and her sister, Maria, president of Ponzi, have grown the business from 16,000 cases in the 1990s to more than 45,000 cases today. Ponzi is one of the largest winemaking operations in the Willamette Valley, and they've managed to expand without sacrificing the quality and high standards set by Luisa's father, Richard Ponzi, one of Oregon's legendary pioneer winemakers. And what is probably too obvious to require mentioning (but we will anyway), Luisa has achieved this amazing success even though she is a woman working in a very male-dominated industry.

The Ponzi winery sits on top of a magnificent hill in Sherwood, Oregon, halfway between Portland and McMinnville, and as we drive through an oversized gate and up, up, up to a gloriously sleek, contemporary winery building—one of the most modern we've seen in all of Oregon—we are excited to meet with Luisa and hear how she has managed to

Sisters Maria and Luisa Ponzi are
continuing their parents' legacy.

by telling us about the most obvious of her vineyard challenges—ones that her father never faced. "I'm working with some of the oldest vines in Oregon," explains Luisa. "Their trunks are gnarly and about as thick as my waist. Some are almost as old as I am and there are a whole set of different challenges, learning how to balance the vine with age."

For example, the older the vine, the less fruit and the more tannin it produces. "They are changing the character of our wines," Luisa admits, "and I don't want to see our signature wine style change drastically because the vines are aging, so it's a real issue for us. We've been asking a lot of these vines and these soils for the past 30 years. From my experience in Burgundy, I know that vines of this age should be giving us something special. In Burgundy, they start replacing vines at 40 and 50 years, but here, I'm seeing the balance in the grape is changing."

Luisa believes one of the key components is to improve the soil, which was hardly a consideration in her father's day. Oregon soil is known to be incredibly fertile, yet the soil in the Ponzi vineyards is different from other properties in the Willamette Valley. "We call it Laurelwood soil," says Luisa. "It's a loess soil that is all basalt based, but its sedimentary soils have been blown over the plains for many thousands of years. So it has a sedimentary topsoil, and then, about twelve feet down, it's basalt. The young vines have a hard time as they only really get the windblown soils, making them very fruity in youth. As they dig farther down with age to the basalt layer, the vines start to pick up

accomplish so much in the past two decades.

The design doesn't try to replicate the feeling of a French Chateau, like so many other wineries around the world. This glass-and-concrete structure, with its impressive set of stairs and bocce court on one side, reminds us more of a contemporary art museum than a winery and is a testament to the grace, elegance, and refined minimalist style of Ponzi wines. So, our first impression of Ponzi Vineyards is that we've arrived at a world-class facility.

The lovely dark-haired, youthful-looking Luisa greets us warmly and then directs us to a small anteroom adjacent to the massive tasting room, which is being set up for a wine-tasting dinner that evening. Luisa is gracious and welcoming as she pours her 2013 Chardonnay Reserve and answers our questions. She begins some real minerality and complexity." But the older vines have drained the earth and Luisa has to consider soil amendments and natural fertilization to revitalize the health and vigor of the vineyard.

Her Parents Were Hippies

Rejuvenating the soil was not a problem Luisa's father had to consider when he brought his young family to Oregon from Los Gatos, California, in 1969. Richard Ponzi was a successful engineer, with one of the most entertaining jobs we could possibly imagine: he designed rides for Disneyland. "It was the sixties," says Luisa, "and my parents were very much hippies. Dad had a fun job but they really wanted to get back to the land. My dad is first-generation Italian, so wine was always in his life. He had made wine as a child with his family and even in Los Gatos they were purchasing some local Pinot Noir grapes and making hearty Burgundy, which was unusual at that time. Then my parents went to Burgundy and

Sunrise at Ponzi's Aurora Vineyard.

Alsace and fell in love with Pinot Noir. Soon Burgundy and the region's wines became their passion; they made many trips before knowing they were doing their due diligence. Back in the States, they traveled up and down the West Coast looking for suitable spots to grow grapes. Honestly, they didn't have a clue how to plant a vineyard, it was more 'Let's do something fun with our family!'"

Dick and Nancy Ponzi wanted to grow Pinot Noir, but they could not find a suitable property in California's Wine Country, where Cabernet reigned supreme. The Ponzis correctly assumed the Santa Clara Valley wouldn't work for them and eventually recognized that the Willamette Valley was the perfect climate for their new venture. "We decided to jump in our covered wagon and head north," Dick Ponzi told an interviewer a few years ago. "We were looking for Ken Kesey. We had a piano and four barrels of homemade wine, three

Luscious Pinot grapes on the vine, just ripe for picking.

children, and a bunch of cats and dogs." Their "covered wagon" was actually a propane-powered truck and a wood-paneled station wagon, two signature hippie vehicles of the late sixties. "They got started on a whim, like a lot of the pioneers," explains Luisa. Only a few of the other early winemakers in Oregon arrived before them: Richard Sommer, Richard Erath, and Charles Coury. More families—like the Adelsheims and the Campbells—followed soon after. "It was a crazy idea at the time," admitted Luisa's dad.

Richard Ponzi did a short stint at UC Davis before he purchased 15 acres of strawberry fields in Beaverton, Oregon. Situated about fifteen miles southwest of Portland, the Ponzis were closer to urban life than the other original winemakers. Their choice was purposeful, as Luisa tells us, because the Ponzis weren't just farmers. "They realized the importance of restaurants and their own desire for city life and culture. I think they were more cosmopolitan than the rest of the pack. They understood that though it's fun to make wine," Luisa says, "you also have to sell it, and that was my mother's job."

The Ponzis built a house and planted their vineyard in 1970. While working the fields and tending to his fragile vines, Dick taught engineering at Portland Community College for some 14 years to supplement their income. "We finally broke even in 1984," he said. Three years later, *Wine Spectator* named Ponzi Pinot Noir one of the 100 best wines. That same year, Dick Ponzi was one of only three Americans to be cited as among the world's finest winemakers by Robert Parker Jr., of *Wine Advocate*. Parker wrote, "Everything I have tasted from Ponzi Vineyards and everything I have read and heard about them, I like. First and foremost are the wines, which are made very naturally and in an elegant, subtle style…. Past tasting experiences have led me to conclude this is Oregon's best winery…. Ponzi Vineyards continues to make Oregon's most complex Pinot Noirs." Those were two very heady endorsements, and after 1988, Dick Ponzi never had to take another teaching job.

Trial by Error

Like the other pioneers, the Ponzis had come to the Willamette Valley because it was the same latitude as Burgundy's Côte d'Or, but it can't be overemphasized that they had no idea if grapes would actually flourish where plums, hazelnuts, and cherries were traditionally the main cash crops. These groundbreaking winemakers were literally risking their livelihoods and their families on high hopes and gut feelings.

Nobody knew what grape varieties would grow in Oregon, but most of the early growers started with Pinot Noir, under the assumption that if this grape flourished in Burgundy, it might also succeed in Oregon where the climate was so similar. They also experimented with many other varietals. Dick Ponzi planted his new vineyard with Pinot Noir, Chardonnay, and different types of Alsatian grapes: Riesling, Pinot Blanc, Müller-Thurgau, and Sylvaner.

"They chose well," explains Luisa, "but not so much with the Alsatian varietals (although

Luisa Ponzi sorts through Pinot Noir grapes.

we still have Riesling growing up here). Chardonnay did not succeed, as they started with a very inappropriate clone. So it really was trial by error. My father understood the mechanics of farming but he certainly couldn't get any help from our neighbors who grew hazelnuts. So the first couple of decades, in the 1970s and 1980s, were really a lesson in learning how to farm grapes. Eventually, they found some great and helpful neighbors at Erath, Eyrie, Elk Cove, and Adelsheim."

While most of the first-wave winemakers were completely focused on growing grapes and producing wine in order to support their families each season, the Ponzis looked more to the future and to other possible ventures. With amazing foresight, they turned to beer and started Oregon's first craft brewery. Just as it's hard to imagine Oregon without Pinot Noir, it is even harder to think of this region without craft beer. And that is thanks to the Ponzis. In 1984, they launched BridgePort Brewing Company, the first in what would become a huge local industry.

"That was a whole other adventure where they had to lay the groundwork, pass the laws, and do the work to make the industry happen," Luisa explains. The family ran the brewery for ten years and then sold it in 1995. Today, Oregon boasts more than two hundred craft breweries, making it home to the fourth highest number of breweries in the country, after California, Washington, and Colorado.

The Ponzis were also very keyed in to the food world, perhaps because Nancy Ponzi sold their wines to the best restaurants in Portland. It was the era of the farm-to-table dining revolution and again the Ponzis identified an opportunity. They opened what would become one of the foremost restaurants in Oregon wine country, The Dundee Bistro. "That was another adventure," Luisa explains. "My parents recognized that the food part had to come along with the wine. We'd seen it take off in Portland, but at that time, the whole idea of local food and local wine was something to be explored." We had the pleasure of dining at the Bistro (before knowing about the Ponzi connection) and fell in love with the place, which is centrally located and beautifully appointed, and returned several times during our trips to Oregon. The food was as good as it gets in Portland, which is saying a lot, and the wine list was unsurpassed in promoting local vintages.

"Good food with good wine makes me extremely happy!" says Luisa and we couldn't agree more—it makes us happy, too. "I love that wine can take you to a specific place in the world, in many cases even to a specific person," she adds. "There are very few products that still do that. I love that wine encapsulates a growing season in a certain region and you can taste what happened that year, as opposed to another year."

Our Home Was the Vineyard

"My sister, my brother, and I grew up on the vineyard; our home was the vineyard and we were the work force," Luisa admits with a laugh. "At that time there were literally no migrant workers, like we have today, so we were pretty much relegated to work in the vineyards and cellars. Who else was going to do it? As a child I loved tagging along with my father. Of the three siblings, I was the one who didn't mind getting messy, so I particularly loved the winery part. I helped in the cellar and went along with my mother when she tried to sell wine in Portland. All that stuff was like a great adventure to me. But things changed as we became teenagers; then we hated it."

Because winemaking was so new to Oregon at the time, the Ponzi kids didn't go to school with other children whose parents were

Above: **An aerial view of Ponzi Vineyards.**
Pages 48–49: **Looking east at Ponzi's Aurora Vineyard.**

making wine. Luisa remembers getting singled out because the newly planted vines around her house were each protected by a milk carton. "I would board the school bus and the kids would tease me about growing milk," she remembers with a smile. "At the time it was so bizarre that your family would be making wine that I never wanted to have kids over. I wanted my parents to be like everyone else—a doctor or a lawyer."

Though it was, in retrospect, a wonderful, rewarding childhood, as normal teenagers are apt to do, the Ponzi kids rebelled against the family business. "We wanted to get out of here as fast as we could," explains Luisa. "We all realized how much hard work actually went into the winemaking process and that my dad still had a full-time teaching job until the late eighties. So my sister went into publishing in

New York and my brother into music in Los Angeles. I went to college to study biology and pre-med, thinking I'd be a doctor. I really loved the science part, but when I went to a teaching hospital I realized there was no way this would work for me. It was too sterile and you needed a tremendous amount of empathy, which is something I don't have a lot of."

Though medicine was not to be in Luisa's future, her training in science would prove valuable. "That's when my father suggested I come back and help with the 1991 vintage," she recalls. "He was very clever and put me in the lab, where I realized that winemaking wasn't all just back-breaking work. There was this whole science part that I'd never seen when I was a child. I realized that science could influence this process and enable you to be creative at the same time, which was, I think, what finally got

The fermentation level at Ponzi Vineyards.

me. So I started working full-time and discovered pretty quickly that if I wanted to pursue this I needed to bring something to the table. I had to either get a graduate degree at Davis or go to Burgundy."

Weighing her two options, Luisa chose to move to France (wouldn't you?), the place that had inspired her parents. She settled in Beaune, in the heart of Burgundy, where she continued her education in viticulture and enology. To her delight, she found herself in school with kids who would eventually inherit the best *domaines* in Burgundy. "I got a chance to taste wine in those cellars and I developed a palate," she says. "Tasting the wines of Meursault and Puligny-Montrachet was what awakened me to how great Chardonnay could be."

As part of her curriculum, she apprenticed with M. Christophe Roumier, of Domaine Roumier, and later, with Luca Currado, of Vietti, in Piedmont, Italy. In 1993, Luisa Ponzi was the first woman to earn the certificate *Brevet Professionelle D'Oenologie et Viticulture*. She also traveled extensively throughout the winemaking regions of Australia, New Zealand, Germany, and the United States. But her greatest education in winemaking, of course, came from her father, who also gave her the push she needed to start trusting her own instincts.

In 1996, Dick Ponzi decided to take a vacation, right in the middle of harvest, leaving Luisa in charge and propelling her into a leadership role. "In retrospect, I think that may have been a calculated move to let me prove to myself that I could handle it," Luisa recalls. "At the time, however, I remember some panic."

A few years later, Luisa took over winemaking duties from her father. "A lot of the ways

I approach winemaking are the same as my father's—pay attention to the vineyard but be very hands-off; don't do a lot of meddling," she says. Certainly Luisa has come into her own as a formidable winemaker and businesswoman. She and Maria, who as president oversees the company's sales, operations, and marketing, have grown the Ponzi business from 50 acres of vineyards to more than 130 acres that produce 45,000 cases of wine a year. In 2008, they built a state-of-the-art 30,000-square-foot sustainable gravity-flow winery named Collina del Sogno (Hillside of Our Dreams). Designed by Dick Ponzi, it was one of the first to be certified under the LIVE Winery pilot program.

Luisa takes advantage of technology and vineyard sources her father never had access to in the winery's early years. Still, she never felt the need to make dramatic changes to the style he established. "Don't fix what isn't broken," she says with a shrug. "I see my role not as redefining Ponzi, but as continuing and extending the reputation my father established for making great wines year after year. At the

Harvest time at Ponzi Vineyards.

same time, I am putting my own imprint or style on the wines. My main goal with Pinot Noir is to express the variety, but to also show some complexity. I would say I've maintained my father's style because it is my style as well. I think we both prefer wines that have more black fruit character, are more powerful, and will age for years and years. Personally, I'm also very interested in texture. I love the Burgundy wines from Chambolle-Musigny, with their silkiness, and Volnay with their pretty mid-palate. If I'm trying to attain something, that's what it would be."

But it is with Chardonnay that Luisa Ponzi feels she has made a real impact at the winery.

World-Class Potential

The Ponzis had early success with Pinot Gris, which they planted in 1978. It soon became the signature white wine for Oregon. Chardonnay

Luisa Ponzi tasting Pinot samples.

had never done as well for the region, though it is currently having a revival.

Like our friend Rollin Soles, at ROCO, whom we would meet later in our travels, Luisa is extremely enthusiastic and optimistic about the future of Chardonnay in the Willamette Valley, despite its not-so-fabulous history here. "In terms of Chardonnay, Oregon was pretty bleak twenty years ago," admits Luisa. "Most people who had used the wrong clone pulled out the vines and then replanted with the more reliable Pinot Gris. The Chardonnay clones from UC Davis were perfect for warm weather but totally unsuitable for us due to the tight structure of the bunch, which made the grapes inaccessible and caused rot deep inside. I had known that they made excellent Pinot, of course, in Burgundy, but the quality of the Chardonnay there just blew me away. I came back from Burgundy around the same time that Oregon State University started importing really good Chardonnay clones, such as 76 and 96. That turned everything around. I feel the Chardonnays we are going to make now have the potential to be world class."

Nothing Else Feels Right

Like all of the second-generation winemakers who are now flourishing in the Willamette Valley, Luisa Ponzi is a link between the legacy of her parents and the next generation. Among the Ponzi siblings there are now eight grandchildren. We were curious whether any of them want to follow in their grandfather's footsteps. "We have high hopes that somebody will come back," Luisa says. "It's going to have to be whoever has the biggest passion and gets the education and experience."

In retrospect, Luisa understands that her parents were remarkable mentors. "My father taught me the skills and instincts to make wine, and to make work fun. My mother showed me the importance of balancing family and business, an especially important skill for women winemakers. I only wish I could do it as gracefully as she does."

Not surprisingly, Luisa married another world-class winemaker, Eric Hamacher, "... one of the most skilled in the Valley," she tells us. In 1995, Luisa and Eric founded Hamacher Wines to craft quality Pinot Noir and Chardonnay. It's no wonder that, given the expertise and pedigree of this winemaking couple, Hamacher is featured in a dozen markets and exported around the world, even though the winery produces only about 2,000 cases a year.

Clearly, winemaking is Luisa Ponzi's passion and art. In a 2013 interview with Forbes.com, she was nothing short of poetic when she explained what growing up in the vineyards and making her own wine meant to her. "The rhythm of the seasons in the vineyard and winery are so much a part of me that I can't envision where else I would be," she said, adding, "If you grow up with winemaking, it becomes part of who you are and nothing else feels right."

Ponzi Vineyards' "Arneis."

2014 Arneis, Willamette Valley

A clean, fresh, and expressive white wine; juicy bright lemon and lime flavors such as peaches, apricots, and pears intermingle with more tropical notes of mango and guava. In the background, light accents of chamomile tea, herbs, minerals, and sweet almonds add complexity. The palate is medium bodied but silky and generous without being overdone. Great balance on a long, lingering, smooth palate. Drink now. Awarded 91 points by *Wine Spectator*.

2015 Chardonnay Reserve, Willamette Valley

Made from Dijon clones, only six barrels of this sumptuous wine were produced. Created in creamy new oak, vanilla is noticeable on both the nose and the palate. This cuvée, produced from a single vineyard named Arellana, contained very low yields of chardonnay fruit, creating a toasty wine that is nicely textured and packed with juicy flavors of white and yellow fruits such as plums, citrus, and pears matched to good minerality; high lingering acidity brings up the rear. Awarded 91 points by *Wine Spectator*.

2014 Classico Pinot Noir, Willamette Valley

A very complete wine from beginning to end, with an inviting textured palate and a nose overflowing with sweet, ripe red and black fruits backed with light, creamy notes of oak and very taught red cherries. In the mouth, this wine coats the palate with lush flavors of black cherries, bright raspberries, and strawberries. A light, sweet top layer of creamy oak and buoyant acidity carries the wine to a long finish. The light to medium tannic structure indicates there's more to come in the future.

2013 Pinot Noir Reserve, Willamette Valley

This dark ruby-colored wine has leaping notes of white pepper, cola, and sassafras, melded with fruity/fruitcake notes of plum tart and a black cherry underpinning. Fresher red fruit and forest notes seem to float above the palate. The juicy, fresh, plush, and deeply concentrated fruit flavors sit generously on what resembles a new-world frame. The acidity is well integrated; the wine has layers of fruit that lead to a long, sensual finish. This Pinot Noir has ten years to improve and gain further complexity in bottle.

2013 Aurora Pinot Noir, Willamette Valley

Another single-vineyard offering from Ponzi, this time a Pinot Noir from their gorgeous Aurora Vineyard. A real Pinot Noir of breed, this wine immediately showcases complex secondary nuances of savory mushrooms and an overgrown mossy forest note, a great sign for the future. This is also a telltale indicator of good wines made in a year that suffered a mid-vintage downpour. The successful wines of this unique year initially seem super ripe in the mouth but then catch a refreshing lushness midway through the palate. This superb wine is no exception, and ages well.

PONZI VINEYARDS
19500 SW Mountain Home Road
Sherwood, Oregon 97140
503.628.1227
info@ponziwines.com
www.ponziwines.com

Tasting Room: open daily from 11am to 5:30pm
Tours: available upon request

ERATH

Oregon

PINOT NOIR

Chapter 5

An Alternate Legacy

ERATH WINERY

Dundee

In previous chapters, we've written about Oregon's "second generation" of winemakers— Jason Lett and Luisa and Maria Ponzi—the grown sons and daughters who are now over- seeing the legacy of their parents, the original pioneers. What happens, though, when your heirs are not interested in continuing in the family business? This is a question Dick Erath had to ponder as he contemplated the future of the vineyard and winery he so lovingly built over the course of his lifetime.

Pinot Pioneer

As one of the very first to plant a vine in the soil of the Willamette Valley, Dick Erath has an almost unprecedented reputation among his peers as a kind of rough, tough, and certainly gruff caretaker of Pinot Noir. Erath has had as much, if not more, experience planting vines in this part of the world as almost anyone else. Though he started with a production of just 216 cases in 1972, by 2006, his winery was generating 90,000 cases a year, making it one of the largest operations in Oregon, with a ster- ling reputation for producing top-tier vintages and excellent entry-level, less-expensive wines.

Dick Erath, 1970s.

In 2005, when Dick Erath was turning 70, he had to come to terms with the fact that his two sons, Cal, then 39, and Erik, 41, were not interested in their father's winery. Knowing this, Dick had spent at least a decade pondering what to do with the legacy he'd created from the fertile earth of the Dundee Hills. Obviously, he couldn't just walk away from the business, and because his life story was so ingrained in the history of Oregon winemaking, he didn't feel comfortable selling to a foreign commercial firm as so many others were doing.

Finally, he made a decision.

In July 2006, Dick Erath sold his winery and his name brand to Ste. Michelle Wines Estates, based in Washington State and owned by Altria, an American tobacco and food conglomerate whose holdings included Chateau Ste. Michelle, Columbia Crest, Snoqualmire, Stag's Leap, and other wineries, and whose annual production back then was more than 4 million cases of wine. (According to Ryan Pennington, director of communications for Ste. Michelle Wine Estates, the company's wholesale shipments for 2015 were about 8.7 million cases.)

Erath granted the conglomerate a 10-year lease on his grapes and committed to personally providing two weeks of consulting time in 2007. He did not, however, sell the 114 acres of grapes he'd been overseeing since his first plantings in the late 1960s. "They got my Pinot and my legacy will continue," Dick Erath told a reporter at the time.

Erath still lives part-time in the house he built smack-dab in the middle of his vineyard, overseeing his vines, which run right up to his porch. "I talk to them," he says. "You can tell if they're happy." And if his grapes are happy, then Dick Erath is happy.

How He Built His Legacy

Dick Erath grew up in Oakland, California, and showed an instinct for farming at only five years of age, when he planted corn kernels next to the sidewalk and sat waiting for them to grow. But as a young adult, he became interested in electronics, and after college got a job with Shell Development in Emeryville. He married in 1961 and, oddly enough (considering his future), he and his wife hardly ever drank wine.

His first introduction to wine was a gift from his father, a Zinfandel from Ruby Hill Winery in Livermore, which cost a whopping $1.50 a gallon. Then, at Shell, he was introduced to Pinot Noir with a 1955 Inglenook. It was love at first sip, and Erath has adored and honored the grape ever since.

In 1965, after several failed attempts at brewing beer, Dick and a friend decided to try their hand at making wine. They picked and purchased 800 pounds of Sémillon grapes from Ruby Hill and fermented them at Erath's home in Walnut Creek, California. The wine was decent enough that he decided to plant some grapes in his backyard. "So that's how I got started," Erath told an interviewer, "and I've been making wine ever since."

He was almost 30 when he began attending classes at UC Davis, where he met André

An aerial view of Erath Winery.

Tchelistcheff, perhaps America's most influential post-Prohibition winemaker, who told him to talk to another guy in the class who was also interested in Pinot Noir: Richard Sommer. Not long after, Sommer introduced Erath to Charles Coury and David Lett. The four became friends and spent endless hours talking about grapes. Along with Dick Ponzi (Ponzi Vineyards), this group would become Oregon's first winemakers. Sommer went on to found HillCrest Vineyard, Oregon's oldest continually running winery, David Lett created Eyrie Vineyards, and Charles Coury established the Charles Coury Winery.

Meanwhile, Erath was searching throughout California for a place to plant Pinot Noir. At the time, grapes were growing in California where the warm weather convinced most farmers that anything could flourish. Though that notion works for vegetables and many fruits, it is not so true with grapes. "The best wine comes from when you pick the variety to fit the window and time Mother Nature has given you. And that's really true of Pinot Noir," says Erath.

While other varieties of grapes can be adaptable, Pinot is much more fragile. "It's a very ticklish, feminine grape," he adds. "They call it a feminine variety because it's very demanding and wants to be treated in a certain way in a very small place on this Earth." (Not a very pleasant definition of "feminine," but certainly one we've heard many times from winemakers.)

Before long, Erath gave up on finding land in California and began thinking about Oregon. He was familiar with the area, having driven through the state several times as a kid. His family had lived in Washington State for a few years. Traveling in Europe, Erath recognized the similarity between the hills of Oregon and the great wine-growing regions of France. He realized that the perfect place to grow Pinot Noir might be in the western part of the state, where the climate most resembles that of Burgundy.

Paraphernalia

In February 1968, Erath accepted a job with an electronics company called Tektronix, which moved him and his family to western Oregon. His moving bill was the largest Tektronix had ever reimbursed as it included several wine barrels, listed on the bill as "paraphernalia." While he worked for Tektronix, he spent months scouring the Willamette Valley for land, finally settling on two 6-acre plots in the Eola Hills. Then he came upon a 50-acre plot near Newberg, a former walnut orchard that had been severely damaged by a freeze in 1955, and bought the land for $7,000. His intention was to set up a mobile home on the property, but lack of fresh water forced him to move the family to a logger's cabin on Kings Grade Road. The cabin had no heat and a floor that listed mightily toward the northwest (a fun bonus for his kids, who liked to ride scooters.)

Despite the less than ideal living arrangements, Erath planted his first four acres in 1969, with 26 varieties of Pinot, Riesling, Chardonnay, Gewürztraminer, Pinot Gris, and many other varietals that didn't grow. The Merlot was also a bust. But it was an interesting experiment, as Erath, and the other early settlers, began to figure out which grapes would thrive in Oregon and, equally if not more important, which ones wouldn't.

Romancing the Grape

Starting out, the first winemakers in Oregon were rather idealistic and somewhat romantic in their search for the perfect plot of land, the most excellent grapes, and the best winemaking techniques. None of the winemakers we interviewed ever claimed that, going in, they thought they'd make a lot of money from the venture. Mostly, it seems as though they were in pursuit of a particular lifestyle, which included living off the land and working hard in collaboration with their fellow winemakers. They were trying to create an industry that would work for their families, help the state of Oregon, and be good for the world of wine. Everything they learned they shared, in a collegial effort that made them all better at what they did.

In 1970, Erath helped Jim Maresh put in his first vineyard, on Worden Hill Road. Then he made a deal with Cal Knudsen to develop Cal's vineyard, which enabled Erath to leave the electronics world and devote himself entirely

The vineyards seem to go on forever when looking out from Erath's tasting room.

to his first love. He planted Knudsen's vineyard in the Dundee Hills in 1972.

In the beginning, when he had no grapes to work with, Erath made cherry wine from a cherry he called Black Republican (this was the era of Watergate, so the name had meaning for a liberal Democrat like Erath). His first Pinot vintage was in 1972, with grapes from both Maresh's vineyard and his own. That year he produced 216 cases of Erath wine, including 100 cases of Pinot Noir. In 1974, he began testing non-California clones and helped to import French clones to Oregon. After planting additional vineyards for Knudsen in 1975,

the two formed the Knudsen Erath Winery partnership and received a permit to operate the first commercial winery in the Dundee Hills. By 1982, their production had expanded to 10,000 cases.

In 1983, Dick bought out Cal's interests in the winery (though Cal maintained ownership of his vineyard) and his wine became known simply as Erath Winery. The same year, Erath planted his Prince Hill Vineyard, next door to Maresh's vineyard on Worden Hill Road. And then, in 1984, Erath's Pinot Noir Vintage Select was named Best American Pinot Noir by *Wine & Spirits*—a stellar achievement.

The entrnce to the tasting room at Erath Winery.

After a divorce in 1987 (for which he had to sell some of his land), Erath wound up with full ownership of Prince Hill Vineyards. Erath Winery continued its successful expansion, growing to 35,000 cases by the late 1980s.

Not the Same as Carrots

The main concern of most of the original settlers we interviewed was to grow good grapes and make the best wine possible. As they learned more and more about Pinot Noir, they began to realize the importance of the soil and what it could bring to the flavor of the grape. Dick Erath used to tell a cautionary tale he heard from Dr. Eggenberger, one of his professors. The story was about how, in Switzerland, a new vineyard was planted with creosoted wooden poles to hold the trellises. Five years later, after the grapes were put into production, the wine tasted like creosote. The grapes had inherited the taste of the wood because Pinot Noir is a very sensitive fruit that picks up whatever flavor surrounds it. This is, of course, one of the things that make wine so fascinating. Pinot Noir will taste different from one piece of land to another, which is not the case with, say, carrots or string beans.

The grapes may be different, but of course it is also the job of the winemaker to orchestrate and bring the wine to life. Erath was quite eloquent on this topic when he was interviewed as part of the Oregon Wine History Project™. "I always think that every year we get whatever Mother Nature gives us in terms of the fruit quality and flavor profiles," he said. "It's like a

Inside Erath's tasting room.

musical score and it's up to the winemaker when he brings that fruit into the winery to conduct that score. How are you going to interpret that score? Where are you going to go with it?"

Wine as a Puzzle

The Erath tasting room, about 750 feet up a red dirt hill, is located amid a seemingly never-ending landscape of rolling grapevines. The building used to be where Erath lived with his family, long after that lopsided logger's cabin. To get there, we turn off the main highway and wind our way through what feels like miles of trellised vines. Looking out over the hillside, we can't help but marvel at Dick Erath's stunning viticultural achievement.

The tasting room is about as commercial as they come, a complete 180 from, say, the rustic Beaux Frères or Purple Hands tasting rooms.

Above: **Gary Horner, May 2016.**
Opposite: **Erath's excellent entry-level vintages.**

Gary Horner, the current winemaker, arrives and escorts us to the expansive yet deserted outdoor patio. It's 11am and we have the place all to ourselves, though it's obvious this would make a marvelous setting for a wedding or other festive event. As we sit, Gary points to Dick Erath's home far in the distance. We can barely make out the structure as it is practically camouflaged by rows of grapevines and rolling hills.

Our first two questions to Gary are the same ones we always ask: How did you get interested in wine? And do you remember that first bottle that changed your life?

Gary smiles and immediately responds (as winemakers always do; it's like falling in love— you never forget the first time). "It was a 1954 Grand Cru Burgundy," he recalls. "The story was that it came out of a doctor's cellar in France. I was born in 1954, so perhaps it was destiny. My friend Andre, an avid wine collector, said to me, 'When I pull this cork, this wine is going to live for 60 minutes,' so we went at it. It looked like oxidized Chardonnay. I took it to my nose—it was loaded with violets, floral aromas, and tea. The wine was still alive. That was my magical 'aha' moment."

Gary Horner started his career as a pharmacist, which is when he met Andre, the guy who turned him on to the 1954 Grand Cru and changed the course of Gary's life. After that first sip of wine heaven, the two friends began tasting a lot of other wines. "One day I started to really sense things," Gary tells us, "like different flavors and various nuances, instead of everything being lumped together. I

Here they sell every wine-related souvenir imaginable. (We would be critical of this place had Linda not spent a small fortune purchasing a dozen wooden signs reading, "A Day Without Wine Is Like a Day Without Sunshine," a signature "Erath" iPhone cover with an embossed plastic wineglass on the back that contains a red liquid sloshing around inside, and some delicious artisanal cheese.)

As Linda is packing up her souvenirs,

had been trained as a pharmacist so the science and technology of winemaking came together really easily for me. I looked at wine as a puzzle I could figure out."

While working on his graduate degree, he began making wine at home, setting up a lab and a small winery in his garage. "My first wines were undrinkable," he admits, "but it was a learning experience that spurred me on."

Horner took a short course in winemaking at UC Davis and on his drive back to Seattle, he dropped in on Terry and Ted Casteel of Bethel Heights Vineyard, seeking employment. Though they did not have a position for him, they told him to come back again for the next harvest. Encouraged by the meeting, Gary realized this was where he wanted to be and what he wanted to do. He returned to Seattle, quit his rather lucrative job, sold his house, and moved into a tiny apartment in Salem, Oregon. He soon found work, at $6 an hour, on the bottling line at Bethel Heights. It was the start of his real education in viticulture.

Working at Bethel Heights from 1988 to 1992 provided the big-picture training Horner craved. "It's where I learned what a ripe grape tastes like," he says. "I worked in the vineyard, in the winery, and on the road." Here was also where Gary met Dick Erath. "I was working in the cellar when he introduced himself on a visit. We stayed in touch for years, always open to opportunities, but the timing was never right."

Finally, one day, Terry Casteel approached him and said, "Gary, I can't teach you anything more, now you must leave the nest."

Technology and Intuition

So, in 1992, Gary got a job as winemaker and vineyard manager for Witness Tree Vineyard. He later broadened his production experience at Washington Hills Cellars, in Sunnyside, Washington; Avatar Wine Partner, in Napa Valley; and Benton-Lane Winery, in Monroe, Oregon. During his six-year tenure at Benton-Lane, Gary built a reputation for his unique brand of winemaking, successfully marrying technology and intuition in his quest to produce world-class Pinot Noir. He also bottled his own wine, under the label Destiny Vintners.

In 2003, Gary was working at Benton-Lane. "I was experimenting with different fermenting cap techniques that happened to get the attention of Dick Erath; he was a real tinkerer, always exploring and experimenting. For years we would go back and forth on the telephone," Gary says. "I knew that he was looking for an exit strategy as neither of his sons was interested in the wine business. One day he said, 'What do you think about coming up north to work for me?' Then a bit later he came down to ask me again in person. I was interested but, as I knew Dick was a man who liked to pinch a penny, I had two conditions: 1) he would have to back away from the winemaking and 2) he would have to open his checkbook. And he agreed." So, a decade after their first meeting, Dick hired Gary and, in him, found a kindred spirit who shared his background in science and his reverence for Oregon's unique terroir. It turned out that Gary was correct; this was Erath's first step toward giving up control

Early spring at Erath, with an on-the-vine promise of a great harvest.

of the winery and planning for the future. And he clearly made an excellent choice with Gary Horner.

We're curious whether Gary found it difficult to work for the notoriously gruff Erath. "For me he wasn't a hard guy to work with," answers Gary. "We had a great understanding and he kept his word about the conditions I set."

Gary began to add his own distinctive touches to Erath wines, using the latest technology to bring out the very best expression of Pinot Noir. He carefully selected unique clones that thrived in specific vineyard blocks, especially when it came to making his highly acclaimed single-vineyard Pinot Noirs. At the same time, Gary believed this region was appropriate for many varietals. He continued experimenting with different wine grapes,

smaller batch production, separating clones and vineyards to observe distinctions, and conducting yeast and cropping experiments.

A Smooth Takeoff and Landing

Gary Horner's technique for producing Erath's delicious lower-priced wines is both surprising and fascinating. "We have multiple tiers of quality within our portfolio and we learned quickly that when making large quantities of entry-level wines, there is no way we can sell a bottle for under $20 if we use new oak barrels," Gary explains. "So back in 1999 at Benton-Lane, I started looking at alternatives for making lower-priced Pinots."

Some winemakers will put staves, shavings, or raw chips into the wine to promote an oaky flavor but this often gives the wine a note of raw wood. "I went through an incredible process of evaluating every alternative casement on the market," Gary continues, "and came up with a certain amount of domino-sized wooden blocks of toasted oak that were suitable for Pinot. These dominoes are sourced from fine-grained, air-dried French oak—from the same forest where we source our barrels—and are toasted to our specifications. We put the dominoes into an inert nylon wire mesh bag and secure it to the tank so that it doesn't float on top. The oak is slow to release flavor and aroma, very similar to what you'd experience in an oak barrel." (The idea of throwing wooden dominoes into the wine is still somewhat amazing to us, but as major fans of Erath's lower-priced Pinots—especially Linda, who is far thriftier than Nick—we come down on the side of supporting whatever works this well.)

Gary also uses micro-oxygenation on his lower-tier Pinots. (Micro-oxygenation is a process whereby air is pumped into the wine to make it more immediately drinkable.) "People think that by using micro-oxygenation you are manipulating the wine, especially the delicate Pinot Noir grape," he explains, "but they are unaware that our new equipment is enormously gentle. Of course, the trend today is to not touch your grapes at all, but I can tell you that by not touching them, you are screwing up badly. Wine does not make itself. Yes, Pinot is a delicate grape with delicate skin and pigment, so the controlled levels of oxygen I inject are gentle and minimal. Twenty years ago they simply didn't have the equipment we do today."

If there's one thing we've learned writing our wine books, it's that winemakers have a million different ideas and ways of honing their craft. Gary believes that Oregon is on the forefront of developing a much better understanding of cool-climate winemaking. He also thinks all the winemakers currently working with Pinot Noir owe a huge debt of gratitude to the early creative individuals who came to Oregon in the mid-sixties. "By sharing what would and wouldn't work with others, we don't have to repeat the same mistakes over and over," he says. And this enables him to make the near flawless wines that are most dear to his heart. "I want all my wines to be completely free of any flaws whatsoever," he says with a lot of feeling. "The wines I fell in love with were softer in style, not aggressively tannic, rounded but with great length of flavor. Instead of being a roller coaster on the palate, I want more of a smooth takeoff and landing. I hope my wines reflect that, with pretty red fruits, lifted acidity, and gently lower alcohol." We think they do.

Our takeaway from Gary is that he is willing to do almost anything to ensure that he's making the best possible wine. He tells us he considers himself as less of a winemaker and more of a caretaker of the grapes; if that is true, then, in our opinion, he is a damn good caretaker.

His So-called Retirement

Some people who retire use the time to pursue a hobby like golf or tennis, but not Dick Erath.

As he was winding down his commitment to making wine in Oregon, he was ramping up a new endeavor: to make wine in Arizona, of all places!

Erath's love of Arizona's dry desert climate started many years ago. To escape the cold, rainy weather of the Willamette Valley, he started vacationing in Tucson. In the mid-1990s, he bought a small plot of land in the desert and planted grapes. Some people scoffed at the effort and warned him that he couldn't grow wine grapes in Arizona. Erath just laughed. "They said exactly the same thing when I came to Oregon in 1968," he told a reporter.

In 2004, he planted a 40-acre vineyard just outside the small town of Willcox, in southeastern Arizona, halfway between his winter home in Tucson and the New Mexico border. He chose Willcox after careful consideration, observation, and testing of the soils. He said the place reminded him of Oregon 30 years ago, when winemaking was just starting. At present, there are about 30 wineries in the state of Arizona, the most famous being Caduceus Cellars, owned by Maynard James Keenan, the lead singer of the hard-rock band Tool.

Erath's Arizona vineyard had some unique problems that he'd never encountered in Oregon—such as rattlesnakes. "The reason the rattlesnakes are here is because we have ground squirrels," Erath said. "So we put in owl's nests and the owls eat the ground squirrels so the rattlesnake population won't explode on us."

He also had to deal with a rash of hungry rabbits and deer that all seemed to love the taste of his grapes.

Erath knew that Pinot Noir would not do well in Arizona because it ripens too early. To figure out which grapes to grow in the arid climate, he visited Chile, Spain, and Argentina and then experimented with 16 varietals of big, robust reds such as Sangiovese, Syrah, Zinfandel, Nebbiolo, Montepulciano, and Tempranillo, which seem best suited to the Arizona climate. His first vintage made entirely with Arizona grapes was a 2009 blend called Monsoon Red, which garnered 85 points from *Wine Spectator*, not a bad start for such a unique venture. "Not a lot of people take Arizona wine seriously," said the Grandpa of Pinot, "but I take it seriously." Despite his early success, Erath sold his vineyard to Todd Bostock's Dos Cabezas WineWorks in 2011.

Today, one of Erath's most important ventures and lasting legacies is the Erath Family Foundation, established in 2006, which funds research and scholarships in viticulture and enological science in Oregon's universities. The foundation's mission is to help young people get an education, and to provide practical assistance, such as language classes, for vineyard workers.

Between the work of the charitable foundation and the excellent wines being produced under the stewardship of Gary Horner, Dick Erath has created an alternate legacy that will certainly extend far into the future.

Pages 70–71: **Stunning aerial view of Erath's Willakia Vineyard.**

NICK'S TASTING NOTES

2015 Estate Selection Pinot Noir, Willamette Valley

A light, delicate Pinot Noir with sweet berry fruits, herbs, and mineral accents. Floral and juicy on the medium-bodied palate with a mélange of black and red forest fruits, cranberries, and baking spices. Bright high acidity and light to medium tannins make this lithe and silky-textured wine pair well with fish such as black sea cod. Also perfect as an aperitif.

2012 Prince Hill Pinot Noir Clone 777, Dundee Hills

A wonderful example of Pinot Noir with a ripe, heady mélange of red and black fruits on the nose, and hints of earth, spice, and a nugget of light oak. The wine texture and mouth feel are superb and the bright acidity keeps the fruit buoyant and lively, inviting the drinker to take another sip. Some good tight tannin lurks beneath the liquorlike quality of the dark red fruits. Long and mouthwatering, this wine will perhaps be drinking slightly younger than the 115, but may prove to be more complex.

2012 Prince Hill Pinot Noir Clone 115, Dundee Hills

Erath's single-vineyard and clonal selection wines demonstrate their very serious winemaking side and this cuvée of Clone 115 is a great example. Broad, rich, and lush on the palate, this displays a much more serious depth of ripe black fruits and complexity than their more red-fruited, simpler entry wines. Herby, spicy, and lightly chocolate flavored with exotic silky notes of overripe black cherries and plums, this is a wine with a more solid sturdy structure buried beneath the fruit than the 777; needs a few years in bottle to gain complexity and come together.

2012 Tuenge Pinot Noir, Chehalem Mountains

Grown and sourced from Chehalem Mountain, this wine has a very fruity yet almost weightless character, and just floats across the palate. Both the Tuenge Pinot Noir and the Willakia Pinot Noir best showcase the winemaking talent of Gary Horner at Erath. These two cuvées display a wonderful duality between red and black fruits, but also have a much greater depth and persistence of fruit than any of the other Erath wines. Both are linear, and with their considerable tannins, they deserve to be destined for the cellar. Excellently balanced, the acidity is lively and the tannins are sweet. I love these wines.

2014 Willakia Pinot Noir, Eola-Amity Hills

Erath purchased the Willakia vineyard (located toward the northern end of the Eola-Amity Hills) in March 2014. The property encompasses 298 acres, of which 119 are currently planted; 98 acres are Pinot Noir and 21 acres are Chardonnay. Erath is currently exploring the feasibility of constructing a new estate winery on the site. Compared to the Tuenge, the Willakia cuvée shows more red fruits, a higher tone, and a more pronounced exotic floral element. Medium bodied, the wine's tangy, bold flavors of cranberries, small *framboises*, and red cherries are all matched to high levels of acidity and small, tight tannins buried deep in the fruit, indicating that it shall be superb with extended time in the cellar; give it 10 years.

ERATH WINERY
9409 NE Worden Hill Road
Dundee, Oregon 97115
www.erath.com
503.538.3318
800.539.9463

Tasting Room: open daily from 11am to 5pm
Tours: by appointment only, from 11am to 2pm

ADELSHEIM

CHEHALEM MOUNTAINS
PINOT NOIR

2014

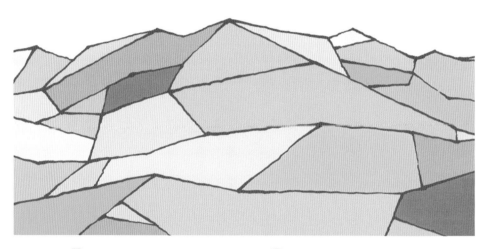

BREAKING GROUND

Chapter 4

An Early Latecomer

ADELSHEIM

Newberg

David Adelsheim likes to call himself a late-comer to the Oregon wine industry even though he and his wife, Ginny, arrived only a few years after Charles Coury, David Lett, Dick Erath, and Richard Ponzi. Adelsheim was, however, one of the few early pioneers who did not move to Oregon from someplace else; originally from Washington DC and Minneapolis, he'd been living in Portland since 1954.

Most of the ten families who first settled here were completely unprepared for the rigors of growing grapes or making wine; only three had studied viticulture at UC Davis or botany at another school. Adelsheim actually majored in German literature at universities in Frankfurt and Berlin and at Portland State University, which is not exactly a prerequisite for either farming or winemaking.

David and Ginny became interested in wine while traveling in Europe in 1969 and, shortly thereafter, decided to buy land in the "country," meaning outside the city of Portland, and began exploring the northern part the Willamette Valley.

A realtor told them that wine grapes had just been planted somewhere in the Dundee Hills, though he couldn't say exactly where.

Later that same day, David and Ginny had a chance meeting with Dick Erath, who pointed to a nearby hill where he had indeed planted a vineyard. Soon after, through a mutual acquaintance, they were introduced to Bill Blosser, who invited them to a May Day party at the home his family was renting in the foot of the Dundee Hills. There they met the Letts, the Courys, and the Ponzis. "So suddenly we knew a great number of the founders of the wine industry," says David, "and we thought, oh well, it won't hurt to look for land where grapes could be planted."

David Adelsheim, 2015.

Seeking the advice of their new friends, they were directed to find a south-facing slope with Jory soil. The Adelsheims apparently were not hindered by their lack of expertise. "Our entire history of farming [at that time] was one garden, one summer," says David, adding with a big grin, "so it was a bit of hubris, if you will."

Buying land back then was a far more naïve process compared to today, where more than 40 years of experience making wines with specific soils and mesoclimates (the overall climate of a vineyard) allow for much greater sophistication and predictability. "In the late sixties, early seventies, if anybody claimed to know anything about the soil or the climates at a site, they would've been considered delusionary." David laughs. "There was no knowledge of what those things meant. The only thing we could do is look at the Yamhill County soil map and realize that the properties we were considering had soil called 'Jory clay-loam,' which was the

Quarter Mile Lane vineyard, 1974.

same soil as at the top of David Lett's vineyard. But anything further than that would presume we had any of the information we have today, which we didn't."

A Leap of Faith

On June 1, 1971, the Adelsheims bought 19 acres in the Chehalem Mountains near Newberg. "And we found we were in the wine business," explains David. "The idea that a new crop could be brought in and planted in this part of the Willamette Valley was revolutionary in many respects. Nobody had ever started a wine business here (as far as we knew). The idea that we would also plant a grape variety that no one knew very well—and in a place no one had ever heard of—was a remarkable leap of faith." That original property was eventually named Quarter Mile Lane vineyard.

Adelsheim, like a number of the other winemakers we met with, told us about the collaborative spirit of the burgeoning wine industry in Oregon in the early 1970s. Information was generously and freely traded. "Without the collaboration of the wine growers, our vineyard would not be where it is today," admits David. "The ten families who made wine before 1980 ultimately crafted something that worked. None of us could have done this alone."

Indeed, when the Adelsheims first planted their vineyard, they called on the help of friends and family. Michael Adelsheim, David's brother and the director of sales before his retirement in 2016, recalls an invitation he received in the summer of 1972. "I got a postcard from David

David and Ginny Adelsheim with their first harvest.

experimental winery of the Lycée Viticole in Beaune, France, for two months in 1974. To expand his knowledge of wine, David worked as a sommelier in Portland and in one restaurant created a wine list with a section devoted exclusively to Oregon wines.

Adelsheim Vineyard produced their first vintage in 1978, with 1,300 cases, including a Pinot Noir they named First Harvest. David admits those 1970s Oregon wines were not always the best. "Even what Dick Graf and Josh Jenson were doing in California at that time was less consistent than what is being produced today," he explains. "The thinking was we didn't want to copy Burgundy, but we also didn't want to make California wine. When we first started, we weren't even thinking we needed acid in Oregon because the grapes would barely get ripe. The idea that you would wait super late and get grapes really ripe never

and Ginny inviting me to an afternoon of back-breaking labor followed by a scintillating feast," laughs Michael.

Ignorance Is Bliss

The original pioneers had lofty ambitions when they started planting grapes in the Willamette Valley. "I think in our minds, we were not out to just make wine, we were out to make *great* wine," David tells us, echoing the sentiments of many of the winemakers we interviewed for this book. "We had absolutely no idea what that meant, but we believed we would get there by planting the great grapes of Northern Europe, and there are exactly three of them: Pinot Noir, Chardonnay, and Riesling."

The Adelsheims planted those three grapes after first building a house on the property they'd purchased. In 1978, they added a small winery in their basement. David developed a close friendship with David Lett and worked at Eyrie, gathering knowledge and experience along the way. He also studied at the

David Adelsheim in his basement at Quarter Mile Lane with his first commercial vintage, 1978.

made sense. However, over the course of the last forty years, the climate here has changed. Today it would be pretty easy to make very ripe, over-the-top wines in Oregon."

Expansion

In 1982, the Adelsheims added a 6,000-square-foot winery adjacent to their house. A second property of 52 acres on Calkins Lane was acquired in 1988, and in that same year, they leased 20 acres across the road from the original 19-acre site. A 120-acre site called Ribbon

David Adelsheim around the time of the vineyard's expansion at Bryan Creek, 1989.

Springs was acquired in 1995. A modern 35,000 square foot winery, built in two stages, in 1993 and 1997, was extended in 2008, adding a sleek new tasting room.

The 2008 winery addition gave the Adelsheims the ability to do a number of things they could not previously do. With more fermenters, picking was not limited to the availability of the tanks. Also, the new fermenters were smaller and movable so that the setup could be more flexible. The Adelsheims could now focus more on single-vineyard and upper-tier wines and start their move away from generic Willamette Valley Pinot Noirs. "It has become critical for us to keep every block of grapes separate through the fermentation and aging processes," David once told a magazine reporter. "Another part of maximizing quality is doing experiments both in the vineyard and in the winery. To maximize the quality of every vineyard block, we need to do comparisons of cover crop use, crop level, timing of thinning, and spray regimens. In the winery, the most important comparisons we can do are those that take place during fermentation. Every experiment we do, whether in the vineyard or in the winery, takes at least two fermenters. The 2008 addition was not really about making more wine. The amount of wine we've made in the last eight years hasn't changed that much. We've stayed between 40,000 and 50,000 cases. However, the mix has shifted from half white/half red to two-thirds red. And 38 percent of that red is now upper-tier, not 6 percent, which is what it once was."

Today Adelsheim Vineyard farms 7 estate

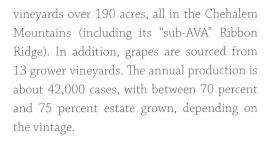

Then and now—the old winery and the rear terrace at Adelsheim vineyard today.

vineyards over 190 acres, all in the Chehalem Mountains (including its "sub-AVA" Ribbon Ridge). In addition, grapes are sourced from 13 grower vineyards. The annual production is about 42,000 cases, with between 70 percent and 75 percent estate grown, depending on the vintage.

Wines That Age

When the early pioneers set out to make wine in this new landscape, very few of them were thinking about how their wines would age. While in France the Burgundians believed their wines had to be pretty difficult to drink when young in order for them to become great in a decade or two, the original Oregon winemakers didn't have that luxury. In fact, most of the them assumed that Oregon wines would *not* age very well. "We were very concerned with how the wines would taste upon release because we had to sell them to stay alive," David explains. "At least for me, I didn't give much thought to how

well my wines would age until the mid-nineties, if not a bit later. That's when I realized the wines that were 10 years old were not only alive but better and more complex."

As we wrote in our chapter on the Eyrie Vineyards, David Lett was the one exception. Lett always believed that his wines would age well but he was virtually alone in his thinking. "David Lett had been saving large amounts, arguably too much, of his own wine," Adelsheim continues. "Once we realized the aging potential of our wines, those of us who were saving two or three cases started to save more. Otherwise we wouldn't have a way to prove to the world what we were discovering: that these wines actually were improving with age. To totally steal the words from Burgundy, with age, the terroir was coming out in our wines. We had set out to make wines that were good at age 3 or 4, and then discovered they were even better at age 10 or 20."

Among winemakers there are a million different opinions about what can be done to improve the aging process. "The more people you ask, the more theories you will get, because fundamentally, we don't understand very well how wines age," David says. "And if anybody tells you they know, they're just making stuff up. But it must have something to do with a climate that is, in some way, cooler. And it may have to do, of course, with picking earlier relative to some gauge of ripeness."

What's in a Label?

Wine labels are an inherently unique art form. Part advertising, part branding, and part artistry, a wine label must be appealing, yet has to separate itself from the thousands of other bottles on the shelf. It must be different but not too different. The label needs to tell the consumer something about the wine in the bottle. If you are shopping for an Oregon wine without knowing anything about the region or what differentiates the numerous wineries, the label is the one marketing tool that will help sell your product. That's a big job for such a small bit of graphic art, so throughout the ages, winemakers have done their utmost to create labels of distinction and originality. For example, Jason Lett paints stunning interpretive visions of his wines and vineyards on Eyrie labels. Rollin Soles incorporates ancient petroglyphs to anchor his wines to the place where they are created. Some, like Patricia Green and Cristom, rely on distinct fonts and the power of their name brand. With Adelsheim, we discovered perhaps the most fanciful concept for a wine label, at least during those early years.

Ginny Adelsheim is an accomplished artist and assumed responsibility for creating a unique look for the family wine labels. Her first idea was to draw a bacchanalian figure and she used a mirror to create the face. The portrait

Early labels depicting Ginny Adelsheim's portraits of people who had helped them create the vineyard, including Eyrie Vineyard's Diana Lett.

ended up looking like a lost relative. For her second label, she set out to draw a different figure, using a friend as a model. Thus was born the idea of using original portraits of family and friends for different vintages. At one point, Ginny even made a label featuring a drawing of Diana Lett, the wife of David Lett, even though Eyrie is one of their competitors.

"The labels were all meant to honor people who had helped us create the vineyard, build the winery, and launch our brand," says David. "And to Ginny, it was important to honor women who often got less credit than their husbands in the wine business. In 1987, we launched a new series, starting with a portrait of our daughter, Elizabeth. Naturally enough, the wine was called Elizabeth's Reserve. Ginny had spent an extended time in Florence, Italy, during which she had seen drawings by the Renaissance painter Andrea Del Sarto. Back in Oregon, she did a drawing of Lizzie in profile in the same style. Since Lizzie was an only child, for subsequent upper-tier labels we borrowed the daughters of some of our best friends."

Though the branding concept was original and instantly recognizable, in 2010, the company decided to redesign the labels for several reasons. For one thing, Ginny's hand-drawn font was difficult to reproduce in later vintages. For another, in selling the wines abroad, the Adelsheims discovered that the image of Diana Lett staring straight out at the viewer was considered somewhat confrontational in Japan. And in the UK, wine merchants felt that the full-color labels looked too "down market" for their higher prices.

ADELSHEIM
YAMHILL COUNTY
PINOT NOIR · 1993
Elizabeth's Reserve

ALCOHOL 13% BY VOLUME

Ginny Adelsheim's portrait of their daughter, Elizabeth.

"Redesigning a label that has been around for 30 years is always a difficult process," David said at the time of the relaunch. "On the one hand, many consumers know us only by our iconic labels. Conversely, many of the gatekeepers in the wine trade view those same labels as a liability. The labels were so distinctive that no one had a neutral opinion. So any new design would, automatically, not be as easy to spot as the labels we were giving up. We were, in essence, hoping for something that was a little more neutral, a little less demanding of attention, more in keeping with the decor of an expensive restaurant. The new labels were envisioned as a 'refreshing' of the previous packaging, while better defining the different tiers for consumers and the trade. The new labels

Pages 82–83: **Adelsheim's Bryan Creek Vineyard.**
Above: **Vintages with Adelsheim's redesigned label.**

and Oregon Pinot Camp. Adelsheim was given the industry's highest honor, the Lifetime Achievement Award, in February 2012 by the Oregon Wine Board (which he helped bring to life and on which he served for eight years, appointed by Oregon's governor).

In the course of his company's 40-year history, Adelsheim has been the vineyard manager, winemaker, and the person in charge of sales, marketing, accounting, and fixing broken plumbing. In 1986, he gave up his duties as winemaker to focus on the overall direction of the company. His principal responsibilities now are strategic and financial planning, marketing and sales, overall direction of vineyard and winemaking activities, and granting interviews to curious but grateful book writers.

Restrained Winemaking

Today the winemaker at Adelsheim is Dave Paige, who arrived in 2001. Paige developed his interest in wine while working at a wine

are classic, elegant, understated, distinguished and, above all, maintain the artistry that has defined Adelsheim Vineyard for four decades."

The company has gone through other profound changes in the past 40 years. Jack and Lynn Loacker joined the company as partners in 1994 and the arrangement has worked out better than anyone anticipated. The Loackers were not only wine lovers but fans of Adelsheim wines in particular when they became co-owners. "David Adelsheim is the epitome of Oregon wine," says Jack Loacker.

As one of the founders of the Oregon wine industry, David Adelsheim has led work on clonal importation, wine labeling regulations, establishing statewide and regional industry organizations, and the creation of such events as the International Pinot Noir Celebration

**Ginny and David Adelsheim with
Lynn and Jack Loacker.**

shop in Ohio. He moved to California to enroll in the viticulture and enology program at UC Davis, where he earned his fermentation science degree in 1989. Dave's diverse experience has included time at wineries in the Sierra Nevada foothills, Napa Valley, Australia, and Monterey, California.

While making Pinot Noir at two wineries in Monterey, Dave traveled to Oregon many times to compare wines and ideas with other Pinot producers. On one such trip in 2001, he and Adelsheim discussed their shared belief that restrained winemaking methods lead to greater complexity and balance. Paige joined Adelsheim that year, just in time for harvest, and since then has brought an open-minded approach and a willingness to combine new and old techniques in pursuit of classic, elegant wines. "Everybody here feels a part of the process of trying to make the best wines possible while still reflecting these vineyards as honestly as possible," explains Paige. "What I love about a great wine is how complex it is and how, for instance, you could be having a second glass and still finding something new and fascinating about that wine. Those are the kinds of wine we are trying to make here at Adelsheim. We are still discovering what it is about the grapes we have in the northern Willamette Valley that is so inherently interesting to us, whether it is some fascinating note of cherry from the Pinot Noir or some floral or citrus component from the Pinot Blanc. We are trying to bring that out in the wine and not hide it or overpower the fruit. We want our wines to have an interesting texture and level of expression, but never at

Adelsheim's current winemaker, Dave Paige.

the expense of what we loved about the grapes to begin with."

An Amazing Time for Oregon Chardonnay

The future of Chardonnay in the Willamette Valley is a recurring topic with Oregon winemakers, and David Adelsheim is no exception. "I was having a long conversation with Josh Bergström just this morning about why Pinot Gris was planted, and we both agreed that it was planted because Oregon was not succeeding with Chardonnay in the eighties and nineties,"

David tells us. "I don't know if it was somewhat related to the clones we planted or how we made the wine. Chardonnay is a wine that is heavily influenced by the winemaker, much more so than Pinot Noir. And it takes people some time to learn the restraint required to make great Chardonnay. We could argue about why we were not succeeding with Chardonnay, but over the last ten-plus years, we've entered an amazing age for Willamette Valley Chardonnay. Now we have these really smart people planting grapes in first-rate sites. And in another ten years, it seems hard to imagine that we won't be making Chardonnays that have the same kind of attention our Pinot Noirs have today. I believe there is greater Chardonnay being produced in Oregon today than ever before, by more people. We are getting much closer to a Willamette Valley-style of Chardonnay that the world will approve and support."

As to future plans for Adelsheim Vineyard, David explains that there would be a "gradual change of management to younger people who want to maintain independence, meet continual challenges, and collaborate in order to raise the bar on Pinot Noir. The idea of collaboration must be uppermost in people's minds. Inclusivity—not exclusivity—is key."

From Vine to Table

In a video posted on his website, David Adelsheim pays tribute to the art of winemaking. "What I love about the wine business is that there is a very direct connection between the grapes in the vineyard, through this very complicated process all the way to the dining table and the person pulling the cork and tasting the bottle of wine," he says. "It's a direct connection; it's really not possible with any other product for most people, but wines have that connection. We certainly hope people explore the story behind our wines, come and see us, look at our vineyard, taste the grapes on the vine before harvest, and explore the connection between the place, the people who are doing the work, and ultimately that unique vintage that makes that wine impossible to replicate.

"We are still true believers in the unique pleasures of Pinot Noir and the amazing white wines of Oregon's North Willamette Valley. The singular climate and the inimitable sites of this place are what allow us to create these memorable wines. It falls to us to explain their seriousness to the world."

Opposite: **Elegantly set tables await their guests.**
Above: **David Adelsheim**.

2014 Willamette Valley Pinot Noir

Adelsheim makes a superb entry-level Pinot Noir, which is a medium-bodied and sleek but reliable wine with some nice floral notes and a light spicy complexity sitting on the seamless palate. Entry-level wines of high quality with little vintage variation are ultra important. It's the first wine that the consumer tastes, so it had better be good. This wine will be excellent in 6 to 7 years; it earned a well-deserved 92 points from *Wine Spectator*; 15,712 cases were produced.

2012 Zenith Pinot Noir, Eola–Amity Hills

Produced from a warm vintage in the valley, this wine still retains great vibrant freshness. There's a good sheen of oak here, and the purity of the fruits benefit from the uplifting acidity. Powerful tannins provide structure, and the wine is long in the mouth and direct. This is a clean and fresh Pinot with hints of spice and vanilla aromas that bring the wine to a long juicy finish. Needs some extended cellar age to soften the tannins and come together. Awarded 91 points by *Wine Spectator*; just over 200 cases were produced.

2012 Boulder Bluff Vineyard Pinot Noir, Chehalem Mountains

Sourced from a plot of land about a mile east of the winery, this is usually a much more red-fruited wine than the Zenith and a style that I prefer. However, my guess is that the warm vintage played a big role in determining the wine's character. Mouth-filling and meaty, this spicy, powerful black-fruit wine is light on its feet. A racy acidity underpins the ripe black cherry and blackberry piquant fruit and small dense tannins. This medium-bodied and mineral-centric wine contains the region's requisite high-toned acidic profile, and boasts a long toothsome finish. It earned 94 points from *Wine Spectator*; 445 cases were made.

2013 Nicholas Pinot Noir, Chehalem Mountains

Produced from the weird 2013 vintage, which was very hot but suffered or was refreshed if picked either before or after the rain. Those who picked last actually made superb wines that open with a warm-climate vibe. (I personally prefer the cooler, even wet vintages as I feel they prove more complex with bottle age.) This wine seems more open and textured than the two previous cuvées, but leans toward a dark-fruit spectrum with earthy mineral hints. Drink in 6 to 10 years. A high-quality wine, it earned 93 points from *Wine Spectator*; 188 cases were made.

2012 Quarter Mile Lane Pinot Noir, Chehalem Mountains

My favorite wine of all the Adelsheim single-vineyard cuvées, this is fresh, sleek, incredibly complex, and delicious to drink. Red fruit-centric, the ripe, sweet berries take center stage. Cherries, raspberries, loganberries, and red plums caress the palate while more complex notes of minerals, spices, and almonds sit in the background, keeping the tannins suitably buried by the fruit. The acidity is well needed and appropriately racy and high. The tannins are structured and the finish is endless and mouthwatering. Needs bottle age 8 to 10 years to integrate properly, gain extra complexity, and soften. The Quarter Mile received a well-earned 95 points from *Wine Spectator*; 60 cases were made.

ADELSHEIM

16800 NE Calkins Lane
Newberg, Oregon 97132
503.538.3652
info@adelsheim.com
www.adelsheim.com

Tasting Room: open daily from 11am to 4pm
Tours: call or email at least 24 hours in advance to make reservations

Beaux Frères

The Beaux Frères Vineyard

2014

Pinot Noir

Unfined & Unfiltered

Chapter 5

The Holy Grail of Pinot Noir

BEAUX FRÈRES

Newberg

The Pinot Noirs of Beaux Frères are among Nick's favorite vintages, and were his introduction to the wines of the Willamette Valley. When we started planning our trip to Oregon, Beaux Frères was at the top of our list of wineries to visit. The quality and consistency of their wines combined with their connection to one of the foremost names in the industry have made Beaux Frères one of the seminal wineries in the valley and a must-see stop on any wine tour of the region.

The winery itself dates back to the late 1980s. Michael Etzel arrived in Oregon almost two decades after the original ten families who settled here, but his impact on the valley has been significant. The winery he created back then retains a middle-of-the-woods rustic quality, yet it has evolved into a world-class facility producing exceptional wines without any conceit. It's a signature vision and an attractive proposition to any wine lover.

In 1986, Etzel was working as a wine wholesaler in Colorado when, on vacation in Oregon, he decided to visit some of the up-and-coming wine regions. He chanced upon a foreclosed 88-acre pig farm for sale on Ribbon Ridge in the northern Willamette Valley, Yamhill

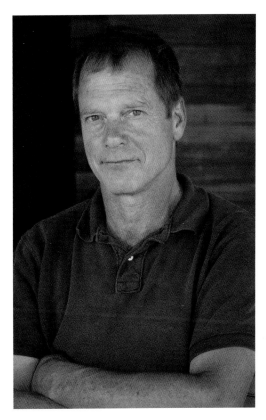

Michael Etzel.

County region. After some deliberation with his brother-in-law, the wine critic Robert Parker Jr., the Etzels bought the land (with financial assistance from Michael's sister and

Parker). The initial idea was to turn the property into a vineyard.

Robert Parker Jr. is married to Etzel's older sister, Patricia, and they live in Maryland with their daughter, Maia, and several bulldogs and basset hounds. He is, as everyone in the wine world knows, one of the most prominent and well respected wine critics of his generation. For a quarter century, Parker has written and published the *Wine Advocate*, and is the author of 12 best-selling books about wine. Though Parker never reviews Beaux Frères wines in any of his publications, his connection with the winery is a well-known secret that, early on, propelled it into prominence. The relationship gave Etzel's burgeoning vineyard a stamp of approval and instant recognition unmatched by any other winery in the area. And Parker's enviable mailing list was exceptionally helpful, to say the least, in selling the wine. Though never blatantly advertised,

Parker's association with Beaux Frères also helped validate Oregon as a wine region of esteem. However, with or without Parker's connection, it must be acknowledged that it was the quality of the wine that put Beaux Frères in the vanguard and on top of any wine lover's "best of Oregon" list.

In 1991, the Canadian commercial developer Robert Roy was approached to become a third partner in the winery, and his expertise in business and financial management has proven to be an enormous asset. There are now two vineyards—the 23-acre Beaux Frères Vineyard and the 10-acre Upper Terrace, planted in 2000—which together produce around 105 tons of grapes per year. Another 20 tons of grapes are brought in yearly to supplement the estate fruit.

Former Pig Farm and Clover Field

After purchasing the farm, Michael Etzel uprooted his family (including his three young sons) from Colorado and moved to Newberg in the summer of 1987. He began his focused pursuit as a vineyard manager by planting only Pinot Noir. It was originally his intention to just grow the fruit, not make the wine.

The first few years were difficult as Etzel slowly built his vineyard. To supplement his income, he took on jobs as a tree feller and a pig farmer, and worked four harvests at Ponzi Winery. In 1990, he sold his first crop of grapes to winemakers Ken Wright and Dick Ponzi, saving just enough to make one barrel of wine himself. In 1991, after Robert Roy joined the

Planting vines on Ribbon Ridge in the late 1980s.

Rescued by Mikey Etzel, Pork Chop has
become a beloved family member.

team, the pig farm was renovated into a winery and Beaux Frères (the name is French for
"brothers-in-law") was created.

With each new vintage, Etzel's efforts
unveiled a Pinot Noir that was the purest
expression of his vineyard. Consequently, Beaux
Frères established itself as a winery of distinction, without ever abandoning its original rural
charm. Most wineries of such prominence soon
invest in creating a glamorous tasting room,
oftentimes selling such merchandise as signature wine stoppers, artisanal cheeses, and
etched wineglasses. In contrast, for a very long
time, Michael Etzel refused to even open a tasting room. Those who came in search of a Beaux
Frères tasting were chased off the property.
Even today, anyone interested in visiting the
winery must first make an appointment.

Follow Your Heart

Today, stately Douglas fir trees cover nearly
50 acres of the farm, with homestead and
winery buildings occupying another 8 acres.
The vineyard is situated on 30 acres (24 of

which are planted) of steep, contiguous south-
east-, south-, and southwest-facing hillsides.
Currently the vines range in age from 15 to 29
years old and are predominately a mixture of
own-rooted Pommard and Wädenswil clones
interplanted with several Dijon clones on phyl-
loxera-resistant rootstocks.

Since their first vintage in 1991, the Beaux
Frères philosophy of winemaking has remained
the same: to produce a world-class Pinot Noir
from small, well-balanced crops and ripe,
healthy fruit that represent the essence of their
terroir. In pursuit of these goals, the vineyard
is planted with tightly spaced vines, and yields
are kept to some of the lowest in the industry.
The grapes are harvested when physiologically
(rather than analytically) ripe. Their approach
to winemaking is based on biodynamic farming and minimal intervention.

"We receive numerous questions about the

Aerial view of Beaux Frères vineyards.

Freshly harvested Pinot Noir grapes.

way in which we make Pinot Noir. It's no different than what thoughtful Burgundians have been doing for decades," explains Etzel. "Pinot Noir is very fragile and needs to be protected from excessive exposure to oxygen. Hence, the winemaking style, once in barrel, is called reductive—meaning its exposure to oxygen is intentionally reduced to the bare minimum. All of this is aimed at preserving the character of our terroir, the personality of the vintage, and the quality of the wine." Etzel's non-manipulative, uncompromising methods guarantee a wine that is the most natural and authentic expression of the vineyard possible. Previous

vintages demonstrate that these techniques also allow Beaux Frères wine to develop significant perfume, weight, and texture in the bottle.

"I have been truly blessed in life, more than once," says Etzel. "It was the summer of 1986 and with little thought about this life-changing decision, my wife and I decided to purchase this 88-acre run-down pig farm in Oregon. The humble beginnings of Beaux Frères began with the financial help of my sister and brother-in-law. With only pure determination, coupled with an exceptional plot of land, the outcome of our decision 25 years ago has been beyond my wildest dreams. I guess there is a value in following your heart over your head."

Biodynamic Farming

"Biodynamic farming, with all the soil aeration, helps refine the tannins, to give you the highest-quality tannins that carry the delicate fruit from mid-palate to finish," Etzel once told a reporter. "This illustrates to me the benefits of farming biodynamically." Etzel is a proponent of the teachings of Rudolf Steiner (1861–1925) who is considered the godfather of biodynamic farming. Steiner was a highly respected Austrian philosopher, social reformer, architect, and proponent of esotericism. Way back in the early 1900s, Steiner recognized that the yields in German farms decreased once farmers changed to artificial pesticides and commercial fertilizers. He deduced it was because the chemicals were manipulating the plants in the wrong way and advised local farmers to let their plants do what they had always done naturally. Thus "biodynamics" was born. Biodynamic farming treats the fields, woods, plants, wetlands, animals, and people on a piece of agricultural land as a self-contained, self-sustaining organism and is now practiced on more than 350,000 acres in 47 countries.

Biodynamics became popular in California during the 1970s and late 1980s. Devotees believe that there are lunar and astrological influences on soil and crop growth and they plant, cultivate, and harvest based on the phases of the moon, the constellations of the

Michael Etzel, 1980s.

Planting vines in 2011; all farming at Beaux Frères is biodynamic.

zodiac, and vineyard water tables. Farming specifically revolves around the Earth's lunar cycles. Days are split into four divisions—leaf, root, flower, and fruit. Farming of each division is predetermined by the calendar. Steiner prescribed nine different preparations to aid fertilization. One example is making use of an ancient practice of burying a cow horn full of specially treated manure deep in the ground to help plants and seedlings establish themselves. It is left to decompose for the winter and then recovered in the spring.

At Beaux Frères, Michael Etzel buries such horns over the winter in a specially selected trench with the ideal shade, pitch, and proximity to stream water. He also makes teas, sprays, and potations of dandelion seeds, yarrow flowers, and other plants to apply to sick vines. The dandelion seeds are fermented in a cow's intestines and the yarrow flower in a pig's bladder.

"We're working with the whole picture," Etzel explains. "Instead of wanting to kill everything that competes with the grape by using chemicals, as was the idea in conventional farming, we respect everything in the vineyard. We try to maximize every natural thing we have."

Of course, some people think biodynamic practices are just plain weird relics of the far-out sixties. For this reason, Beaux Frères wines are not marketed as biodynamic. "We don't want people thinking we're a little nutty," says Etzel.

Where a Wine Begins

Situated just off the main road, Beaux Frères is an unpretentious, rustic winery, which is surprising when considering their reputation and output. A small sign points up the private road

The very unassuming tasting room at Beaux Frères features a Greek amphora.

that leads to the winery, which is on the first floor of what still looks like a converted barn. As we drive up, we see a huge black pig sauntering toward our car. We soon learn her name is Pork Chop, and Linda's dog, Bernie, confused but curious, is about to make friends with his very first porker.

It's pouring rain in Newberg (big surprise!) as we enter the small and, again, very unassuming tasting room, which is basically a wooden bar, a few bottles of wine, and a bench. Decorations are minimal, to say the least, consisting of a few framed photos and geological maps hung on the wall. A large Greek amphora sits off to one side and that's about it for décor. This is quite a stark difference and a refreshing change from the elaborate French-style chateau or contemporary steel-and-concrete tasting rooms we're used to seeing in California (and that we later saw in many Oregon wineries as well).

We have an appointment to meet with Mikey, the middle son of Michael Etzel's three boys, who is now 33. Moments after our arrival, Mikey enters the tasting room wearing rain gear and chomping on a sandwich, followed by several very large and very wet dogs. We can tell at once that he is somewhat uncomfortable being interviewed; he tells us we really should be talking to his dad (even though his dad specifically requested that we talk to Mikey). But he soon seems to warm to us, escorting us up a flight of stairs into a beautifully appointed conference room where, he points out, his dad did much of the handsome woodwork. Mikey begins the interview by telling us how Beaux Frères came into being.

Mikey Etzel.

"When my dad moved our family to Oregon, we represented the second wave of 'pioneers' who were attempting winemaking in the region. This was after David Lett and Elk Cove and all the others," Mikey explains. "This property was a foreclosing 80-acre plot that farmed a variety of crops, including clover, over the past 100 years. The winery itself was

The conference room showcases beautiful furniture handcrafted by Michael Etzel.

originally a dairy farm, but when we arrived, it was being used as a pig barn. We started planting in 1988 and 1989. When I was young, there were 30 or 40 vineyards in this part of Oregon; now there are over 500."

Early on, Mikey discovered that establishing a vineyard was very hard work, and he watched the long hours his father devoted to the place. "You have to be willing to be a bit of an engineer at the winery, to do the service work on the equipment yourself. And you can't just be a weekend farmer," he adds. "You're constantly tinkering."

He discovered he enjoyed life in the vineyard and the work fascinated him. "One great thing my father taught me was a good work ethic," he says. "Throughout my life, I've always worked hard in the vineyard. I like growing things. The vineyard has always fascinated me because this is where wine begins. I feel that the understanding of this process is invaluable."

Michael Etzel gave his boys little jobs

Michael Etzel.

around the vineyard to earn their allowances, as he once told a magazine reporter: "They worked at open houses as ticket collectors and glass washers. As they got older, they did mostly vineyard work in the summers, spreading straw, making compost, pruning, or doing trellis work. If they needed spending money, they had to earn it. I always hoped they would want to get involved, but when they were in high school, they didn't demonstrate any interest in the wine industry. It was just a way of life for them. It wasn't until they left and went to Europe that they said, 'I think this is what I want to do.' Being a child once myself, I never enjoyed being told what to do, so it wasn't a dictatorship, like, 'You're gonna follow in my footsteps!' Certainly, my wife doesn't believe in that. She believes they should pursue whatever passions fill their hearts and minds."

As young adults, Mikey and his brother Jared worked for other wineries, such as Cristom, Brick House, and WillaKenzie Estate, and eventually traveled to Spain and France to explore winemaking on the other side of the Atlantic.

"My palate was not appreciating wine when I was young, at least up until I was about 19 and did a harvest in my freshman year in college in Rioja and Priorat (in Spain)," says Mikey. "Those experiences totally opened my eyes for the first time. Spain was amazing. The vines there grow on sheer rock. Their 1,000-year-old winemaking methods and culture are still in use—they don't use any machines and they wear these little baskets tied at the waist. I was entranced with how they did things, and

The rustic sign is barely noticeable from the road.

training in these regions was a big component in my education. When I came back to the States I enrolled at Oregon State University, which, at the time, had a new enology and viticulture program. I enrolled and found that my primary interest lay in vineyard management."

Land in Oregon

Returning to Oregon, Mikey gained vineyard experience at several other wineries and in 2012 began working for a new company formed by a movie producer named Mark Tarlov, who had recently sold his interest in Evening Land Vineyards. "He then started an innovative project called Chapter 24," Mikey continues, "and I was the winemaker there

for two and a half years under the guidance of the legendary Burgundian winemaker and producer Louis-Michel Liger-Belair. Without a doubt that was among my most important learning experiences to date and the one I most appreciate and cherish. The most amazing and wild aspect of Chapter 24 was their ability to source fruit from 30 to 40 different vineyards all across the valley. It's a very ambitious project, and during that time I really got a chance to explore in detail each terroir of the valley."

Studying the various terroirs in the Willamette Valley had to be an eye-opening experience for the young winemaker. One of the things that most interests us about Oregon is that, even today, there is so much farmable land available. "We are not like Burgundy for

There are few sights more beautiful to a wine lover than grapes hanging on the vine.

many reasons but probably one of the most vital elements is the French AOC rules about expansion," Mikey tells us. "It's impossible for someone to just come along and plant a new vineyard in Meursault; the government designates the regions' barriers and all the land is taken. There is no expansion, period. Here in Oregon—within this 90-mile stretch of valley—one can plant a vineyard anywhere. There is so much unchartered territory out there, even with our substantial growth as a wine-producing region."

This is such an interesting point for us because, in addition to there being available land, it can be purchased at a fraction of the cost per acre compared to almost anywhere in California, particularly Napa or Sonoma, which is totally out of reach, cost-wise, for all but the richest corporations or conglomerates. Anyone at all interested in starting a vineyard or acquiring land in a winemaking region should obviously begin their search in Oregon.

The Holy Grail Style of Pinot Noir

In July 2015, Mikey returned to Beaux Frères. "Dad and I felt it was about time to attempt to work together, as I'm dedicated to carrying on the family legacy," says Mikey. Jared Etzel, the older son, is currently working at a winery in Napa and though Nathan, the youngest, often helps out in the vineyard, he is an engineer working outside the wine business, at least for the moment.

When the question of how the wines at Beaux Frères have changed over the years arises, Mikey thinks carefully about his answer. "One change from the early days is the percentage of new oak in each blend," he explains. "When my father started out, he used a much higher percentage of new oak (barrels) and a heavier toast. They ended up making these brooding wines that were more masculine than what we produce today. That profile is similar to the early years of most winemakers, where they want their wines to stick out from the rest. I think our American culture and palate is tuned in to a new-world style of winemaking: that is, 'big' wines with obvious sweetness. But now there is a niche for consumers who appreciate our wine, and that's where we land. The Eola-Amity Hills have this great terroir that constantly produces what I think of as the Holy Grail style of Pinot Noir, the main characteristic being bright, saplike fruit."

According to Mikey, Beaux Frères will continue to produce small quantities of elegant wine, as they are unwilling to lower their standards to increase production, like so many other wineries have done. Expansion almost always comes with certain drawbacks, and loss of quality is usually first and foremost. But that is not about to happen at Beaux Frères.

For Mikey, and for the rest of his family, winemaking is an art and a science, with just a touch of something divine. "Because we started Beaux Frères from scratch, with little money, we were forced to do all the menial jobs ourselves," explains Mikey. "We didn't have employees; we *were* the employees. And now we can afford it, but that still doesn't keep us from doing the tasks. You have to know every detail it takes to get to the end; you can't do that from an office." He is proud to be a second-generation winemaker and follow in the footsteps of his father and uncle. Beaux Frères winery is a family operation and will remain so for the foreseeable future.

Finally, we ask if Mikey is worried about his dad retiring anytime soon. "Fully retired?" he responds with a laugh. "Never!" And then adds, just in case we haven't yet figured it out ourselves: "Plus, it's pretty damn fun working together."

There's a world of wisdom in the Etzels' dog Earl's eyes.

2013 Gran Moraine Chardonnay, Yamhill-Carlton

I rarely come across this wine, so it was a treat to taste it. The grapes were sourced from the Gran Moraine Vineyard in the Yamhill-Carlton AVA. The wine has a dark golden color and a revolving door of aromas that jumps from the glass. Youthful, the wine's subtle but expressive bouquet brings forth strong scents of pear, orange rind, melons, tangerines and floral notes framed in well-judged sweet medium oak. Lighter, more complex tropical aromas of pineapples, mango, custard, vanilla, and spice make an appearance. This wine bounds along with a fruity, ripe, dense palate that contains powerful mineral notes paired to high bracing acidity that holds up the heavy, waxy (honeycombed) texture of the broad palate; shows excellent balance. Richly fruited, it's a medium-bodied wine, yet expansive, with a long, lemon-lime citrus finish.

2013 Guadalupe Vineyard Pinot Noir, Dundee Hills

Wow! The light transparent ruby color foretells the style of the rarely seen, single-vineyard, high-altitude-grown wine about to come. Bountiful, pure, sweet scents of red fruit leap from the nose. Fresh and bright, this medium-bodied wine is all about the Côte de Beaune, with flavors of sappy raspberries, ripe red cherries, cranberries, and strawberries all wrapped up in super-high acidity. The palate is smooth and sleek with a seamless quality and the finish is uplifting with a late arrival of a mineral spice note. All told, 162 cases were produced from the McMinnville AVA planted on volcanic soils.

2013 Hyland Vineyard Pinot Noir, McMinnville

This wine has a medium-dark ruby color followed up immediately with an almost pungent red and black high-toned fruited nose (which blew off).

The wine exudes notes of piercing red cherry, raspberry, and cranberry aromas intermingled with black cherry and cassis fruit, adding flesh to the lightly oaked frame. Racy in the mouth and medium bodied, it has a nice smooth texture. There's a great dimension to the silky fruits, and a huge electric surge of noticeable acidity that runs throughout this wine, leading to a good long finish. This rarely seen cuvée made from vines planted on volcanic soils shows much more of a black-fruit profile than the Guadalupe cuvée; 97 cases were made.

2015 Beaux Frères Vineyard Pinot Noir, Ribbon Ridge

The flagship wine from Beaux Frères's originally planted estate vineyard is always a stunning bottle of wine, even in difficult vintages such as the 2013, where halfway through the warm perfect year it rained heavily. It is a touch lighter in color than usual but still retains its beautiful complex nose of bright, high-toned red cherries accompanied by streaks of darker notes such as forest floor, damp earth, and cola spices supported by a medium lick of sweet oak. This is not the typical meaty, exotic, dark-styled Beaux Frères cuvée, but rather a more delicate, fresher, and subtler rendition due to the vintage conditions. Still, this is a nice wine, which will radically change over extended time in bottle. The profile is medium bodied and lighter than usual, but the wine still has complexity, sweet supportive tannins, and very high acidity matched to decently ripe fruit. It also has a very respectable depth of fruit and should age well. Drink within 10 years, but best in 5 to 8. A total of 2,194 cases were produced; awarded 95 Points by *Wine Spectator*.

2014 Beaux Frères Vineyard Pinot Noir, Ribbon Ridge

Produced from a more consistent vintage, this cuvée is quite the opposite of the 2013, expressing a livelier attitude and a richer and more complex fruit concentration; it's as if everything has been ramped up a notch. It presents a youthful medium-ruby color with hints of crimson, and an explosive, youthful nose packed with a mélange of red and dark forest-floor fruits covered in a sweet, light sheen of vanilla oak and floral aromas. Soft, generous, and sleek, this wine coats the palate, cramming in earth, mineral, and cinnamon flavors with the ripe fruit. A complex and complete wine; herbs plus an excellent high acidic balance keep the fruit in check, and grainy, powerful tannins ensure a good future. The finish sails on and on from this juicy, serious expression of Pinot Noir. In all, 2,450 cases were produced; earned 95 points from *Wine Spectator*.

2008 Beaux Frères Vineyard Pinot Noir, Ribbon Ridge

This wine has taken on some wonderful harmony inside the bottle since its extended bottle age. All the separate components, tannins, acidity, and fruit have melded beautifully, and this is now a very graceful, elegant, and complex wine. Secondary nuances of mineral, spice, and floral aromas and an attractive mossy, earthy note all join together. Long in the mouth, this wine soars with laser beam high acidity and is supported by good tannins. Drink now through 2018. From a warm vintage, 2,500 cases of this wine were produced; awarded 93 points by *Wine Spectator*.

2007 Beaux Frères Vineyard Pinot Noir, Ribbon Ridge

A taste from the cooler 2007 vintage is an interesting comparison to the warmer 2008. Though much more delicate than the 2008, I liked this wine. It was very pretty and complex in an inviting way. The bouquet is gentle and fragrant, with notes of silky red and black fruit paired with notes of aged, fading, autumnal leaves, meat juice, sweet tobacco, and loamy earth. The wine is fully open, soft, contemplative, and mature, with a light body, fine tannins for structure, and of course the region's high natural acidity. It's starting to drink superbly, so consume over the next 5 to 7 years. A total of 3,500 cases were produced; awarded 92 points by *Wine Advocate*.

2014 Cuvée 1959 Pinot Noir

There's a minute production of this special, rare cuvée. The wine displays a very dark ruby color accompanied by a seriously powerful cornucopia of numerous aromas that positively bounce around and soar from the glass. Forceful notes of rich, ripe black and red small fruit dance among more complex notes of buried vanilla pod, Lapsang tea, meat juices, spice, and licorice. Medium bodied but with a superb depth of silky smooth fruit, this wine reveals an impeccable pinpoint balance of fruit to acidity to sweet, strong tannins. Indeed, everything in this wine is seriously ramped up, and it certainly has a long future ahead; yet it still manages to remain elegant, graceful, and light on its feet, for a wine with so much power (in Pinot terms). More black-fruit than red-fruit flavor, this is a commanding wine that will need considerable time to resolve its separate components, ease up, and gain complexity. It's all there for the future. Only 475 cases were produced.

BEAUX FRÈRES

15155 NE North Valley Road
Newberg, Oregon 97132
503.537.1137
info@beauxfreres.com

Tours and Tastings: by appointment only; contact the winery at tastingroom@beauxfreres.com or 503.537.1137.

Pinot Noir

Willamette Valley

DOMAINE SERENE

EVENSTAD
R E S E R V E

GROWN, PRODUCED AND BOTTLED BY
DOMAINE SERENE, DAYTON, OREGON, USA ALC. 13.1% BY VOL.

Chapter 6

The Only Oregonians Making Wine in France

DOMAINE SERENE

Dayton

If you were to ask us which winery to visit while you were in Oregon and only had time to do one tasting, we'd send you directly to Domaine Serene in Dayton. Not only would you be sampling the very best that Oregon has to offer, but you'd also be doing so in one of the most stellar tasting rooms and winemaking facilities we've ever seen in the United States, and that includes some of our Napa favorites.

The story of Domaine Serene is both an insider's view of how this part of Oregon became the quintessential Pinot Noir producer in America and a love story worthy of a Hollywood blockbuster. If ever there was a prime example of the value of the contemporary adage, "Follow your passion," which we read in every women's magazine and hear on every talk show, it is the life story of Grace and Ken Evenstad.

A New Challenge

Both Ken and Grace grew up in Minnesota, and met in 1966, when Ken was studying pharmacology at the University of Minnesota.

Grace was living in an apartment with two other women, one of whom was named Serene. When Ken's date for the big spring dance got sick and had to cancel, Serene, a friend of Ken's, convinced Grace to go on a blind date with him. "Ken arrived and we went to the formal," says Grace, "and by the end of the evening we were madly in love with

Ken and Grace Evenstad, July 2013.

Aerial view of Domaine Serene's Winery Hill Estate.

each other." They soon married and moved to Alaska, where they had two children: Serene, in 1967, and Mark, in 1969.

Wine was not really familiar to the Evenstads until they were adults. Both Ken and Grace grew up in homes where their parents didn't drink, and it wasn't until they were living in Alaska that Grace tasted wine for the first time. "Ken's fraternity brother from Livermore, California, was living in Anchorage and always had wine with dinner, which was new to me and Ken. My

very first wine was a bottle of Wente," recalls Grace. "I fell in love with the idea of having wine at dinner and we were enjoying some pretty decent California wines in Anchorage. Then we moved back to Minnesota and were able to get our hands on a greater variety of wines at a shop called Haskell's, which still exists. Within two years, we'd worked our way through a lot of different wines and then focused on Burgundy. By around 1972, we were talking about having our own winery someday."

Their dream was to produce Pinot Noir. "I first discovered Pinot Noir through Burgundy," explains Ken. "I began to study and taste a lot of Burgundies and it was about that time that I said I think we should try to make an American Pinot Noir that can challenge the French Burgundies."

Like many couples who think about making wine, it was a dream that had to be put on hold while they raised their family and Ken built his pharmaceutical company, a job that kept them locked in to Minnesota. "Not many people know this, but you can't move a pharmaceutical company," Grace tells us. "Once you have a drug that's approved for manufacture, it's approved in that specific building. If you move your company, you lose the ability to make all of your products. It takes years to get re-approval."

Twenty years later, in 1989, the Evenstads were visiting friends in Dallas, where they enjoyed a fine bottle of California Cabernet. "We also ordered an Oregon Pinot Noir off the wine list," remembers Grace. "We fell in love with the quality of the fruit in that bottle of Oregon wine. Once we tried it, we never wanted to go back to Cabernet, which seemed so simple and uninteresting. On the way home, on the plane, Ken turned to me and said, 'Someday we should have a winery and a vineyard.' I replied, 'Well, honey, our somedays are running out.'"

Her answer surprised, and delighted, him. "I'd been working on her for 20 years and met with a lot of resistance to even thinking about seriously doing it," says Ken. "At this point in time the kids were raised and she was looking for a new challenge, so she took me up on it."

Princess of a Grape

They made an appointment with an Oregon real-estate agent and, the following weekend, were flying west to look for a vineyard. Ken had done some reading and knew he wanted to be in the Dundee Hills. There happened to be an available parcel—42 acres which had recently been logged. When the Evenstads went to inspect the land, it was enshrouded in fog and they could hardly see the property. Still, they decided that, if the soil tests proved positive, they'd buy it.

It took great vision to make this leap of faith. At the time, the Willamette Valley was a virtual newcomer to the winemaking business. And the property the couple was considering was an absolute mess. Logging is not kind to the land and had left behind huge piles of rocks and stumps covered with poison oak and scotch broom. Clearly, it was not going to be easy to prepare the land for planting or for construction of the house they wanted to build.

Yet the Evenstads were undaunted. When the soil tests proved the land was more than suitable, they forged ahead, determined to turn their vision into a reality. "After we bought the property, we returned about two months later when it was not socked in by fog," remembers Grace. "We couldn't find it because we hadn't known what it looked like to begin with. And when we finally did discover it, we realized we had this fantastic view."

Despite the view, they faced some serious challenges when it came to readying the land.

Domaine Serene's first facility in
McMinnville, circa 1990.

Early on, they brought in Joel Myers to help out. "When Ken and Grace first looked at this property, Grace was literally climbing over stumps and logs. You really had to use your imagination to envision it becoming a farmable piece of vineyard property," says Joel.

For several years the couple commuted from Minnesota to Oregon. Ken continued to work as president of Upsher-Smith Labratories, his pharmaceutical company, and had very little time to spend on the vineyard, so initially, Grace did most of the work. "And that had not occurred to me when I agreed to the vineyard," says Grace with a laugh.

When they started making wine, the Evenstads decided that a blend of vineyards would be their core, and thus they planted a variety of clones of Pinot Noir rootstocks. They wanted different elevations within their property and different-facing slopes. They used a facility in McMinnville and produced their early vintages there. Their first wine was bottled in 1990, made with contracted fruit as their own grapes were not yet planted.

Grace had worked very hard to make the wine and then was appalled when Ken suggested she had to sell it. "It was almost like selling a baby," she explains. "I'd put my heart and soul into it. It was all done by hand and I really didn't want to part with it."

The effort and love they put into their winemaking paid off royally when their first release received 90 points from Robert Parker Jr.—quite an accomplishment for a brand-new label. It gave them fresh encouragement.

Realizing they'd outgrown their McMinnville facility, they purchased a building in Carlton in 1994 and converted it into a winery. "And that was where we really launched our Domaine Serene brand," explains Ken. "We set out to make a world-class Pinot Noir and as it turned out, the fruit was so exceptionally pure that the wines began challenging some of the Grand Cru wines in terms of quality."

Only a handful of places on the planet have the right combination of conditions—climate, rainfall, and other natural elements—needed to grow Pinot Noir grapes, and Oregon is one of them. "Pinot Noir is such a delicate princess of a grape, it knows everything you've done to it and it remembers," says Grace.

Gravity Flow

The Evenstads were sustainable farmers long before it became popular to use the word *sustainability*. They have always favored natural products over harsh chemicals. They maintain low crop yields, and they leave more than half their land in its natural state to encourage wildlife and flora. They also dry farm all of their vineyards. Cover crops and tillage are used to manage soil moisture. "When you don't irrigate, the vines go very, very deep for moisture and other nutrients," says Ken. "This makes a healthy and sustainable vine, because in the years where there is less rain, the vines can go down farther in the soil for more moisture."

Soon the Evenstads purchased more land, enlarging their property from 42 acres to more than 200. By 1999, they had three vineyard estates and more grapes than they could ferment in the Carlton facility. They began thinking about building their own winery on their property. Ken sketched his first ideas for a gravity-flow winery on a napkin, which now hangs on a wall in the winery.

"That was a very exciting time," recalls Ken. "Grace and I wanted to build a landmark winery here in Oregon and nothing before had been done quite on this scale." They certainly succeeded in creating an outstanding contemporary facility that works extremely well for Pinot Noir. The building boasts five levels for gravity flow, which means the grapes and the wine are moved by the force of gravity instead of pumps. Pinot Noir is a fragile grape that does not like to be handled, punched, or pushed, and gravity flow helps retain the quality of the fruit.

The sorting line is inspected by a number of people as the grapes pass down the conveyor belt. These are then de-stemmed and moved into fermenters. The red wines are pressed off

Grace and Ken Evenstad on the gravity-flow sorting line.

and put into barrels, and aged in the barrel cellars until it's time for them to be bottled. "We need at least twice as much space as any average producer requires," explains Ken. "The wine remains in barrel for up to two years and then we find it is very important for it to stay in the bottle for at least a year before it is released. Pinot Noir fluctuates in bottle a lot that first year and then things even out. Most of our wine is sold in restaurants and we want to make sure that when people order and open our wine, it is tasting good."

Inside the winery, where the grapes are transformed into wine.

A Watershed Moment

At a wine auction in Naples, Florida, called the Naples Winter Wine Festival, the Evenstads purchased a lot that included an 18-year vertical of Domaine de la Romanée-Conti La Tâche, one of the best labels that the Domaine de la Romanée-Conti (also known as the DRC) produces. When they finished the tasting and were on their way home, Grace said to Ken, "We should put our wines up against the DRC. I think we have a good chance of winning in a tasting."

It was a bold move to have their three wines—1998, 1999, and 2000 (Grace Vineyard, Mark Bradford, and Evenstad Reserve)—compete with the DRC's 1998, 1999, and 2000, but the Evenstads were confident in their wines— though understandably nervous as there was a lot riding on the outcome.

The tasting took place during an Oregon wine camp that brought a lot of professionals from around the world and 22 states to the region, including two master sommeliers, and some French wine buyers as well. It was a completely blind tasting, even for the people pouring the wine. In the end, after everything was tallied, Domaine Serene won first, second, and third place for the 1998 and the 1999, and first and second for the 2000. "It was a very big and very exciting day for us," says Grace. "We realized we were not only world class but we were better than the benchmark Pinot Noir for the world. It was a watershed moment."

The Evenstads continue to challenge themselves. One of their most innovative new wines is Coeur Blanc, which means "white heart," a white Pinot Noir made from gently pressing their largest Pinot Noir grapes. "We get just a squirt of white juice from the center of the berry with no skin contact and from that we ferment in barrel like we would a Chardonnay and make this wonderful product that has not

Above: **Domaine Serene's Grace Vineyard.**
Pages 114–115: **At sunset, the woolly mammoth statue seems to come alive.**

been made in the United States before," says Grace. "Everything in the wine business seems to be a never-ending learning experience."

"We're not just in the business of making wine," says Ken, "we're in the business of making outstanding wine." And they are succeeding. Domaine Serene just scooped up one of only thirty-one platinum "Best in Show" medals at the 2016 Decanter World Wine Awards with their 2012 Winery Hill Vineyard Pinot Noir, outperforming 6 Grand Cru and 26 Premier Cru Burgundies. After 16,000 wines were tasted, Domaine Serene received a total of eight medals.

These are only a handful of the numerous awards garnered by Domaine Serene and one of the reasons why the wine is distributed throughout the world. Nick was quite a fan even before we arrived in Oregon, having tasted their wines many times in London.

A Beautiful Place to Visit

A long driveway weaves through the Domaine Serene property and takes you past a huge sculpture of a wooly mammoth, reminiscent of the animals that once roamed this ancient land. The tasting room is expansive and elegantly appointed, probably one of the top three most sumptuous tasting rooms in all of the Willamette Valley (with Archery Summit and Ponzi being our other two favorites.) On the day we arrive, we are treated to an amazing afternoon with the very knowledgeable Cody Newell, the hospitality manager for Domaine Serene.

After an extensive tour of all five levels of the winery (which left us gasping for breath), Cody sits us down to a table overflowing with crystal wine goblets. Pouring us a sample of the 2012 Récolte Grand Cru Chardonnay, Cody

**Our extended tasting with Cody Newell
required the use of many glasses.**

has been designed with one thought in mind: Is this best for the wine?"

Cody cites the 2014 harvest as one example of how Ken's ingenious design leaves nothing to chance or circumstance. "The 2014 vintage in the Willamette Valley has been recognized as one of the hottest ever. The harvest was so huge that people were using custom crush facilities and having portable fermentation tanks delivered to their wineries. Some had tons of extra fruit on the vine, some even had to turn down their contracted growers. Many said, 'We simply don't have space, so we have to take something out of barrel that really should sit for four more months.' Those were the kinds of situations Ken and Grace—with great foresight—managed to avoid with their new design and with methods that were put into place so that those challenges could be anticipated."

Such meticulous preparedness for the obstacles that can be thrown at a winemaker is what makes Domaine Serene so special. Every inch of the winery is carefully created and immaculate, and nothing is left to chance or circumstance. This quality of perfection shines through in the wines, which are brilliantly crafted, expressive, and absolutely flawless. The Evenstads are producers of such pristine wine that we doubt anyone would be disappointed after opening a bottle of Domaine Serene.

The Only Oregonians Making Wine in France

draws an interesting comparison between Ken Evenstad's health-care business and wine-making enterprise. "One thing that always concerned Ken, even at Upsher-Smith, where he was designing heart drugs," explains Cody, "was to focus on doing something that was going to help someone. If not, he didn't want to release it. And he brings that same approach to the winery. I mean, every aspect of the winery

One of the things we noticed while traveling

through the Willamette Valley is the influx of French companies buying up wineries here. Ever since the Drouhin family arrived in the 1980s, French winemakers have been interested in Oregon. We suppose that's only natural, considering the similarity between French Burgundy and Oregon Pinot Noir. Yet at Domaine Serene we discovered that this trend is being flip-flopped by the Evenstads.

In April of 2015, Ken and Grace expanded on their original vision of winemaking by purchasing Château de la Crée, a Burgundy wine estate in the Côte-d'Or, which includes a unique collection of vineyard sites, a contemporary gravity-flow winery, and a restored chateau in Santenay, which dates back to the 15th century. "Owning and farming legendary vineyards in Burgundy is a dream come true for us," says Ken. "We have a once-in-a-lifetime opportunity to make our own wines from famous vineyards like Morgeot in Chassagne-Montrachet, Clos des Angles in Volnay, and La Garenne in Puligny-Montrachet, where world-class wines have been made for centuries." The couple plans to bring the Château de la Crée brand to new markets, including the United States. (Thanks to Cody, we were lucky enough to taste the 2011 Chassagne-Montracht, Château de la Crée Chardonnay, which was mind-bogglingly good.)

The Evenstads also want to encourage a crossover of information and techniques between the two wineries. "The Burgundy harvest is very short," Grace tells us when we ask for a specific example. "It's one of the things we are hoping to improve. They harvest everything in a week, from the highest to the lowest elevations. Chardonnay and Pinot Noir, in seven days! We want to pick everything at the perfect moment of ripeness. It's going to be more difficult and cramped because they have a labor shortage over there."

Nick likes to write about clones (which are the particular rootstocks of the grapes) though Linda thinks the topic is far too technical for the average reader. But when we ask Grace about the clones at Château de la Crée, her answer is unexpected. "Well, they don't even know what their clones are over there," she explains. "They've mixed lines for so many centuries, they don't know what the rootstocks or the clones could be." We suppose it shouldn't be a surprise, considering they've been making wine at Château de la Crée since before Columbus set sail to prove the Earth was round.

Grace Evenstad hosts a tasting in the caves at Domaine Serene.

Last, we wanted to know if the Evenstads had plans to expand into other parts of the world that are making wine. "No," Grace said. "We are in Oregon because of Pinot Noir and we're also excited about our Oregon Chardonnay. We're in Burgundy because of Pinot Noir and Chardonnay. This whole business is really about our passion for these two grapevines."

This latest endeavor in France brings Grace and Ken a new opportunity to further develop their expertise with their favorite varietals and to "discover" a new terroir from the place that inspired their passion for winemaking 25 years ago. They've come full circle and we can see that it's been a marvelous ride for them and a treat for those of us who get to enjoy their spectacular wine.

Sunset at Domaine Serene's Evenstad Estate.

2012 Récolte Grand Cru Chardonnay, Dundee Hills

A wonderfully opulent Chardonnay, superbly complex and a real delight to drink. This is the estate's unspoken but highly prized nod to a European Grand Cru-style Chardonnay. Exuberant and Moorish, this white wine is broad and expansive on both bouquet and palate. The nose is packed with fresh aromas of clotted cream, peaches, and wild white flowers. Vanilla and white truffles soon waft from the glass. The palate is equally inviting, broad and sweetly spicy, displaying layers of pear, citrus, grapefruit, and peach flavors. The wine's balance between acidity and fruit is expertly brought together after spending 18 months in sweet oak, 75 percent of which is new. It has a long lime-tinged finish. Drink now through 2019. All told, 250 cases were made. This vintage earned 93 points from *Wine Spectator*.

2015 Clos de Lune Vineyard Chardonnay, Dundee Hills

An unabashed yet lighter, more "modern" version of the Récolte Grand Cru Chardonnay and a great example to boot. A shiny reflective gold color leads to an attractive bouquet of citrus and pears that mingle with more exotic fruit scents of guava, papaya, banana, and ginger, all sitting on a lightly oaked vanilla-flavored frame. Medium bodied, silky and smooth with a soft texture, this wine has an excellent floaty finish that just keeps on going. Acidity is high but exquisitely balanced. Seems like a blend of new- and old-world Chardonnay. Drink now through 2020. A total of 120 cases were made; awarded 93 points by *Wine Spectator*.

2012 Côte Sud Vineyard Pinot Noir, Dundee Hills

This cuvée sees 16 months in French oak, 68 percent of which is new and perhaps is the reason why the wine reveals quite an exotic nose, exuding wild spices, ripe black fruits, and earth. The oak is perceptible but not intrusive and the tannins are big-boned and tight yet sweet. The wine has an amazingly smooth, liquorlike texture with overtones of coffee beans. It's silky but has inner richness, a good depth of fruit, and tangy supportive acidity. This wine is a not only a winner but also long-lasting. Drink now through 2018. Production totaled 384 cases.

2012 Mark Bradford Vineyard Pinot Noir, Dundee Hills

With the attributes of a Burgundian Pommard, this is the firmest Pinot in the Serene portfolio. This west-facing vineyard utilizes a Pommard clone, and the resultant wines are the most masculine, sturdy, and brawny of all the cuvées. Dry and powerful in structure with sinewy, chewy tannins, black tea, black fruits and smoky accents matched to high acidity, this is a formidable wine and not short on fruit or aging potential.

2015 Evenstad Reserve Pinot Noir, Willamette Valley

Always a favorite and a wine I drink regularly. Simply said, it combines excellent winemaking and complexity with a lip-smacking flavor. Despite being the most international in style of all the Domaine Serene wines, the cuvée is still varietally focused and, most important, red fruit-centric. Overflowing with taut, bright fruits and light spices, the wine is sleek, smooth, and silky, yet retains a wonderful juicy, natural sweetness. It is immediately accessible due to its sweet, caressing tannins. Delicacy and concentration combine to make this the quintessential example of an Oregon Pinot Noir. In all, 1,500 cases were produced; awarded 91 points by *Wine Spectator*.

2006 Grace Vineyard Pinot Noir, Dundee Hills

Another perfect example of how Oregon Pinots manage to superbly come together with time and age in the mid-term, this wine was excellent, complete, and very tasty. All the components of acidity, generous fruit, and tannins have melded together. Sometimes Oregon

Pinots are criticized for being tasteless and unexpressive when young, but this wine shows they open beautifully after a few years in the bottle. Ripe and generous with a cornucopia of red summer fruits, the finish is long and complex. With 150 cases produced, this vintage earned 93 points from *Wine Spectator*.

DOMAINE SERENE

6555 NE Hilltop Lane
Dayton, Oregon 97114
503.864.4600
866.864.6555
www.domaineserene.com

Tasting Room: open Friday and Saturday from 11am to 5pm and Sunday to Thursday from 11am to 4pm
Tours: offered twice daily at 11am and 2pm by appointment only, with a minimum of 72 hours' notice; limited to 8 people

2014

OREGON

CRAFTED

P H

PURPLE HANDS

Pinot Noir

LATCHKEY VINEYARD DUNDEE HILLS

Chapter 7

A Youth Spent in the Vineyard

PURPLE HANDS WINERY

Dundee

We were unaware of the winery called Purple Hands when we first arrived in Oregon (actually we were unaware of many of Oregon's great wineries before that initial trip). The story of how we discovered Purple Hands and its connection to two of the legendary pioneers of Oregon winemaking, Ken Wright and Rollin Soles, is why we found the Willamette Valley such an extraordinary place. As wine lovers will agree, the excitement of finding a great new winery is what makes a wine tour so much fun.

Our story starts at Domaine Serene where we first heard the name Ken Wright; this was purely by chance, luck, or destiny—whatever you want to call it. We were enjoying a tasting when we noticed the cover of a local wine magazine depicting a bottle of Domaine Serene next to one from Ken Wright Cellars.

We wondered: Who was Ken Wright? And why, if his wine was featured so prominently on the cover of that magazine, had we never heard of him?

We did some quick research and discovered that the *Oregon Wine Press* had recently put Ken Wright on its cover and included a long article about his remarkable success. We

learned that his was a very highly respected name in Oregon wine.

Even though our time was booked solid with tastings and interviews, we headed over to the Ken Wright Cellars tasting room in Carlton. Once there, we were blown away by the wines and knew we had to include this winery in our book. Ken himself wasn't there on that Sunday, so we made a note to come back when we could meet with him. Then, during the course of our tasting, we learned that Wright had named two of his vintages after his two sons and that one of them, Cody Wright, was also a winemaker, and quite a good one at that.

We couldn't imagine that Cody could be making wines as excellent as his father's, but we decided nonetheless to go for a tasting because it would certainly make for an interesting story. So, we left the Ken Wright Cellars and headed over to Purple Hands in the hills of Dundee, which was not so easy to find. At the time Purple Hands' tasting room was in a converted old farmhouse on a very dusty, only partially paved road. However, thanks to our trusty GPS (how did we ever find anyplace without them?) we arrived about 45 minutes

Cody Wright with his wife, Marque, and son, Tyrus.

structure that would last for years to come. And it wasn't just the wine: the whole place felt like a tribute to a new brand of winemaking and a new generation of winemakers.

We were impressed with the artistry of the tasting room, which was both hip and welcoming. The distinctive wine labels and etched wineglasses were super cool in a biker-chic way. Even the wall hangings seemed cooler than in any other of the tasting rooms we visited.

We thought, okay, father and son are both making brilliant but entirely distinctive wines—now we are onto something! But that was hardly the only surprise of the day.

Keen to meet and interview Cody, we asked Jacklyn, the hostess in the tasting room, how we could contact him. She kindly wrote down his phone number and email address and, handing the paper to us, said with a smile, "Oh, and you might also want to talk to Rollin Soles, at ROCO, just down the road."

Why was that? we wanted to know.

"Rollin is Cody's stepfather and he also makes amazing wine."

Okay. Now we were hooked, for real.

Cowboy Boots and Purple Hands

Though we had managed to taste the wines of both Ken and Cody Wright, and, later in the trip, of Cody's stepfather, Rollin Soles, we couldn't manage to get interviews with any of them on that first foray to Oregon. So, two months later, in May 2016, we found

before closing. (The tasting room has since moved to downtown Dundee.)

On that first visit, we were a little surprised to discover that this tucked-away winery was packed with patrons who looked like they'd spent the entire afternoon there, enjoying Purple Hands wine. After a quick tasting, the reason was obvious.

Though we'd loved Ken Wright's wines, we were equally captivated by the wines at Purple Hands, which had a personality and point of view completely different from Ken Wright's, yet were quite stunning on their own. This modern fruit-forward wine was lush and drinkable, while also displaying an impressive

Opposite: The Latchkey Vineyard with Purple Hands' former tasting room in the background.

ourselves sitting on the porch at Purple Hands with Cody Wright, sipping his 2014 Latchkey Pinot Noir and getting to know a true artist of winemaking.

Cody is a rough-and-ready cowboy-hat-wearing character with, yes, somewhat purple hands from working in the fields. He was affable but also dead serious when discussing his philosophy and vision of winemaking. Like the sculptor who takes a block of marble and chips away at what shouldn't be there, Cody Wright looks at a vineyard and sees what he wants to pour into a bottle.

A Youth Spent in the Vineyards

His education started early and covered a great deal of territory. Cody was six years old when his parents, Ken and Corby Wright, moved from Carmel, California, to the Yamhill Valley, in Oregon. Previously a partner of Talbott Vineyards, in Salinas, Ken, like many ambitious and forward-thinking young winemakers in the 1980s, was eager to explore all that Oregon had to offer.

In 1986, Ken and Corby founded Panther Creek, which they sold in 1994 after they divorced. Corby would eventually marry Rollin Soles and start ROCO while Ken would create Ken Wright Cellars. So Cody was literally raised between two exceptional wineries. And it was always a labor of love for everyone involved. (Recently, after helping us with some photos for ROCO, Corby sent an email saying, "Great to hear you're meeting with Cody and KWC. It's a family affair of the heart. Or else

we're all just fools of the highest order to be in this business.")

From the age of eleven, Cody was riding tractors and doing punch downs after school. He spent his childhood days wandering among vineyard rows and moving fermenters with forklifts, helping out between classes and during holidays. "I had a good head start because I grew up around the masters, so a lot of my understanding is through osmosis," says Cody. "Whenever I could, during summer vacations for example, I would be out in the vineyards full time. I learned by just standing in front of fermenters." Winemaking fascinated Cody and the feeling stayed with him. He graduated from the University of Oregon in 2003 with two science degrees: one in environmental science and the other in environmental geography. "So I was studying rocks and slopes and dirt," he explains. He worked in various vineyard management and winemaking roles at Argyle, Ken Wright Cellars, and ROCO, and traveled to broaden his understanding. "I went to Australia and made wine for the famous Knappstein winery in the Clare Valley," he tells us. "Then I went to New Zealand and did a vintage at Ata Rangi in Martinborough." Everywhere he worked, he added to the wealth of knowledge instilled in him by his father and his stepfather.

After finishing school, he didn't know what was next. His father wanted him to stay in Oregon and work with him, so that's what Cody decided to do.

But he found himself conflicted. He'd learned a lot about winemaking from his

OREGON

PINOT

NOIR

Le Nouveau Monde

PH

PURPLE HANDS

2014

Gorgeous artwork on the label for Cody's very special and prestigious cuvée; only 100 bottles were produced.

family, his studies, and his travels and it had made him an independent thinker with a longing to experiment with his own ideas and ways of doing things. "Working with these people all over the world had opened my eyes and taught me new techniques and different styles. I wanted to put these methods into practice," he says. "My father, as you know, is a master winemaker and so is Rollin, and I wanted to combine all this knowledge I'd accumulated here and abroad to create my own thing. By that time I was pretty focused on what I wanted to achieve.

I was young but I had been fermenting grapes, making wine, and understanding the concepts behind the process since I was a teenager."

Though he was eager to make his own wines, initially he lacked the funding. "No one gave me money to start Purple Hands," he explains. "I told my father I wanted to make my own wines, try some new techniques, extractions, and experiments. He said, 'You can use the winery when everyone is gone. You can buy your own barrels and your own grapes. I'll let you use the equipment, but you clean all the stuff afterwards. I want the fermenters in better shape than when you found them.'" This was a place to start and Cody grabbed it. "All I could afford at the very, very beginning was some Oregon Merlot and maybe half a ton of Pinot Noir grapes," he says. "So that is how Purple Hands really started, with just myself, in 2005, in Ken Wright Cellars."

Yet he instinctively knew that if he followed his calling, it would take him where he wanted to go. "If you really strive for something and want to go in that direction, doors start opening," says Cody—which pretty well describes his career as a winemaker.

Life Happens in the Vineyard

Though he is only 36 years old, Cody has been around vineyards and wineries far longer than most young winemakers. His approach to winemaking is a reflection of his stunning education combined with his youthful enthusiasm and love of experimentation, though he does confess that sometimes he goes too far. "It

Cody Wright on the porch of his former tasting room.

definitely took a long time to get to this point and I did go through trial and error," he admits. "In 2010 I went on a no-oak-whatsoever bender with maceration. I was going to show everyone that you could gain enough power through whole cluster. But at the time, it turned out that without the development of oak, the wine wasn't quite as powerful as I wanted to see years later."

His absolute commitment to the soil is both profound and poetic. "I work diligently every year to make sure that the soil in the vineyard is expressed and captured in a way that gives the consumer a window into millions of years of Earth's evolution," he explains. "This also combines with showing consumers how elevation shines through. In lower elevations, you have more fruit-forward wines, and in higher elevations, the wines become more mineral driven."

Cody is obsessed with when to pick the grapes, down to the very minute. He loves to talk about "pick time," that optimal moment to bring in the grapes from the fields, and why it's so important. "For me, the pick date is one of the huge factors in determining how a bottle of wine is going to age. I spend so much time in the vineyard trying to find the new personality of the vines and grapes in every particular year," he says. "Tasting, tasting, tasting. Analyzing and just trying to figure out when is the perfect moment for me to pick. You have to watch it very carefully. Life happens in the vineyard and you have to discover that vibrant balance of fruit to acidity. You can miss it, so I take this dead seriously. I also

The tasting room is decorated with
unique and fun objects.

think it is the one defining characteristic that differentiates my wines from so many others made in the valley."

He is acutely aware of the legacy, and his indebtedness to those who came before him in Oregon. "I am lucky to be making wine now that Oregon is famous for Pinot Noir," he says. "I can focus on honing my skills because those guys—the old masters—laid the groundwork. They made no money. They did it because they were passionate about Pinot Noir, and now Oregon Pinot Noir is an institution."

Expansion

Purple Hands started as a one-man operation in 2005 with 250 cases. Cody's wife, Marque, who grew up in southern Oregon amidst timber operations and cattle farms, joined Purple Hands after they married in 2012 and assists in managing the winery business. Not long after its inception, Purple Hands' Holstein Pinot Noir was awarded 92 points by *Wine Spectator*, a rather spectacular feat for such a new winery. People began to take notice and eventually the winery found investment partners in wine buffs Scott and Michelle Campbell of Portland.

Though they are currently expanding, Purple Hands is still a small cult winery. "I'm really the only person making the wine, just me and Marque," says Cody. "I have some really magical family in my life plus my friends who've all really supported me. I work closely with my vineyards. I try to make sure I express what's in the vineyard. So now I'm just doing my own thing, using my own philosophy with the knowledge I've picked up over the years."

His connection to the land on which he was raised has helped in many ways. "I found this site; a vineyard that was never on the market. There was some California interest in buying it but the woman who owned it did not want to sell to an outside conglomerate. She preferred selling it to a native Oregonian." Cody and the Campbells were able to purchase the land in the Dundee Hills.

Today, Purple Hands produces some 5,000 cases a year from six different vineyards. Cody's wines are all "single vineyard" and cost $50 a bottle, which we think is a steal considering the small quantities being made.

In 2016, Purple Hands opened a brand-new facility in downtown Dundee that will take the winery to another level. Not that Cody Wright wants a huge expansion. "I could probably handle up to 7,000 cases at the new facility," he says. "During harvest we get help from the tasting-room staff and some friends, but I think 5,500 is the magic number and I want to focus on quality."

The Future

Though Cody is a Pinot Noir specialist, he is thinking about producing Chardonnay, and perhaps Nebbiolo, in the future. "My favorite red variety next to Pinot is Nebbiolo, a late-ripening grape I'd absolutely love to grow," he says.

Whichever direction he decides to pursue, it is clear that his focus will remain laser sharp. "I don't make wines for anyone else," he says. "I'm just following my own path. I'm trying to make wines that show more dimension. I think that more and more people working within the valley have become interested in my wines because they are different. It isn't so much about creating wine as it is creating depth, precision, soul, and life, while showcasing the vineyard, the special clones we use, and the terroir we are given. I'm looking for focus and clarity, purity and honesty. I've become entranced with sharing my idealism and philosophy with people about winemaking and what I embody within the wines I make."

We're absolutely certain that Cody Wright will succeed and that in the future we'll be hearing much more about Purple Hands. Today, his wines compete with the best that Oregon has to offer. Tomorrow, Purple Hands could surpass them all. Certainly, as a second-generation Oregonian winemaker, Cody is the future of the industry: purposeful, creative, and serious, with a huge dollop of coolness. He sits in the middle of a very important Oregon wine legacy and he is the perfect candidate to carry on the traditions and maintain the high standards of those pioneers who came before him.

Oh, and one other reason we love Cody Wright: as we concluded our visit he offered us an entire case of his wines. No, actually, he didn't offer, he insisted and then went to grab the wine himself. The gesture cemented our appreciation for the guy, and being able to enjoy his amazing wines over the course of the next few weeks only increased our appreciation for his true artistry.

The kid is not only a brilliant winemaker; he understands a thing or two about promotion.

Purple Hands' 2014 Pinot Noirs.

2014 Stoller Vineyard Designate Pinot Noir, Dundee Hills

This is the most accessible of the single vineyards, yet it is no less intense. Showing a full body and decent tannins, this wine has medium-high acidity matched to a mélange of fresh, juicy red and black forest fruits, as well as floral and mineral notes, all wrapped up in a lovely silky texture. Drinking well now, its bottle age has mellowed the wine and its components are coming together, so drink it over the next 4 to 6 years. Grown on Bellpine soils, this is a very good, very enjoyable wine. Only 600 cases were made of this vintage, which earned 93 points from *Wine Spectator*.

2014 Shea Vineyard Pinot Noir, Yamhill-Carlton

This wine displays a bright crimson color, violet hints, and a youthful watery rim. Sappy and inviting, the glass opens with bright red cherry, raspberry, floral, and spice notes. With more airtime, notes of meat pies, black cherries, and forest floor start to emerge, which give this wine quite a complex edge. After a while, black tealike scents and notes of India ink start to intermingle with ripe black cherries to create a complex earthy nose. With a sturdy and compact feel, this wine is another great example of Cody showcasing the vineyard and containing or reigning in the hot vintage conditions. Drink between 4 and 12 years after release. A mere 200 cases were made of this vintage, which earned 91 points from *Wine Spectator*.

2014 Holstein Vineyard Designate Pinot Noir, Dundee Hills

This is my personal favorite of the all the "single vineyard" offerings released by Purple Hands. The Pinot grapes for this wine were sourced from a high-altitude vineyard. Vivid crimson in color, this wine bursts out of the gate, announcing its presence with powerful pure bright traditional Beaune-like scents of crunchy red fruits, raspberries, *framboises*, spices, floral notes, red cherries, and barely discernable vanilla oak. Fresh and pure in the mouth, expansive, with a torrent of small red fruits that coat and fill the palate with a textured sweet elixir of red liqueurlike mineral fruit, light spices, and deep-veined black cherries, this wine has a more overtly mouthwatering fruity profile than the other cuvées. Juicy with tangy high acidity, the wine finishes with a lingering light touch of blueberries. Nicely textured, mouth-filling, and youthful with tight, dense, powerful tannins, this wine has a lot in reserve, and earned itself 93 points from *Wine Spectator*. Drink between 5 and 15 years from release.

2014 Freedom Hill Vineyard Pinot Noir, Willamette Valley

Expresses a more pure red-fruit style than the Stoller, which I personally find more refreshing; vibrant and drinkable when working in conjunction with wines with such inherent levels of high acidity rather than those of the richer, more Côte du Nuits style that are sometimes sought after in Oregon. The Freedom Hill works well in this respect; the vineyard sits higher than the Stoller, at 300 to 500 feet, and has produced a wine with a more hightoned, crisp, and red-fruit feel. It's silky, luscious, and streamlined in the mouth while still being generous and richly fruited. The acidity melds perfectly with the fruit, and with still-buried ironlike yet sweet tannins, it has a good future. Perfect in 6 to 12 years.

2014 Latchkey Vineyard Designate Pinot Noir, Dundee Hills

Bought in conjunction with his father, Ken Wright, this could be the jewel in Cody's vineyard crown. A serious example of an Oregon Pinot Noir, this wine shows a noticeably darker purple color than the other cuvées. It has a youthful bloody crimson rim and is much less opaque, with violet glints; the nose is extremely deep and almost smoky even though the wine is only slightly oaked. The is an expressive, throaty, and spicy wine; black plums and cherries swirl with the more exotic scents of Brazil nuts, minerals, licorice, red fruits, blueberries, weeds, candy floss, and a touch of cream. The palate is super rich for a Pinot, smooth and textured with a wonderful duality between power and lightness. This wine is long in the mouth with buoying high acidity, dense small tannins, and a wonderful core of fruit—all of which ensure future bottle age. Drink between 5 and 20 years from release. There were 420 cases produced from this vintage, which received 91 points from *Wine Spectator*.

PURPLE HANDS WINERY

1200 North Highway 99W
Dundee, Oregon 97115
503.538.9095
cellar@purplehandswine.com
www.purplehandswine.com

Tasting Room: open 5 days a week, Thursday to Monday, from 11am to 4:30pm

KEN WRIGHT CELLARS

SAVOYA VINEYARD

2014

Chapter 8

Mother Rock

KEN WRIGHT CELLARS

Carlton

Opposite: **The KWC labels are photographs of wax carvings made by artist David Berkvam.**
Above: **The tasting room is a former train station.**

As mentioned in the chapter on Purple Hands, we discovered Ken Wright Cellars quite by accident: while visiting Domaine Serene, we came across a *Wine Spectator* issue featuring Ken's wine on the cover. This compelled us to drive to Carlton to visit his tasting room, which, we learned, was in a converted train station with picnic tables on what used to be the platform.

Though Ken wasn't there, we had a lovely tasting and were very impressed with the wines, especially the 2013 Savoya Vineyard Pinot Noir. "I taste green onions," Nick said, gazing at the glass with wonder. We later learned that indeed the Savoya vineyard was planted on a former onion field and the name *Savoya* is Ken's interpretation of the word *cebolla*, which is Spanish for "onion." The 2013 Savoya was the perfect example of what Ken Wright's wines strive to achieve: a connection to the specific piece of land where the grapes are grown.

While most winemakers talk about the importance of terroir, Ken Wright is the strongest proponent of site-specific winemaking we've ever encountered. He was in fact the leader of the single-vineyard movement in Oregon, pushing hard to establish six new AVAs in the northern Willamette Valley, long before some other winemakers thought this was a good idea. Ken also had some very different ideas about winemaking and farming that were fascinating to discover. We learned that he and his wife Karen are very involved in community activities—so much so that by the time we left our interview, after several hours and a lovely communal lunch, we had begun to think of Ken as the unofficial "Mayor of Carlton."

Ken Wright.

Kentucky Blues

Ken Wright hails from the Midwest. His parents were students at the University of Illinois when he was born. Intending to study law, he attended the University of Kentucky in Lexington. A job waiting tables at a continental restaurant called the Fig Tree exposed him to fine wine and ignited his passion. He cleverly convinced the restaurant owner that the servers would sell more wine if they were allowed to taste various vintages. Consequently, one day a week, the wait staff was invited to sample wines from one region on the wine list and this became Wright's introduction to wine. "I fell in love with wine and began making some very bad wine of my own," he says with a laugh.

Wright shared his appreciation for and interest in wine with his roommate Allen Holstein, who was majoring in horticulture. On their own dime, they had been drinking Mateus Rosé (who wasn't, in the 1970s?) until Wright brought home a bottle of Beaujolais, which rocked their world. Eventually they graduated to Burgundy.

The two friends planted an experimental vineyard at the university but the humidity and the pesticides needed to control the insects made it almost impossible to grow acceptable grapes. One day they met a young winemaker named Helen Turley, who told them they could only grow hybrids in the Kentucky soil. Though their vineyard experiment failed, Wright discovered he loved getting dirty in the fields and watching things grow. He changed his pre-law major and decided he needed to be in California. (Allen Holstein would go on to work in the Willamette Valley as vineyard manager at Domaine Drouhin Oregon, Knudsen Erath, and Stoller, and with Rollin Soles at Argyle. And of course Helen Turley would become one of the most famous winemakers in Napa.)

Towing the Grapes

Ken signed up to study enology and viticulture at UC Davis (where Rollin Soles would be his teacher in microbiology) and then went on to work on California's central coast for Ventana Vineyards and Talbott. In California he made friends with such soon-to-be-legendary winemakers as Josh Jensen, Dick Graff, Rich Sanford, Steve Kistler, and Steve Doerner. Graff, the founder of Chalone, invited Wright to join an informal group of winemakers called the Small Winery Technical Society. They would meet for all-day sessions to discuss fermentation techniques and yeast strains, sharing ideas and learning from one another.

"We met at Mount Eden once a month," remembers Ken. "We did a lot of research and work. I was the kid in the group, so I took copious notes and kept my mouth shut and my ears open."

Meanwhile, his former roommate Allen Holstein moved to Oregon in 1979, along with many of California's best young winemakers.

This gave Wright a reason to visit and those trips sparked his interest in the Willamette Valley. One such visit to the Dundee Hills in 1982 convinced him that this was where the finest Pinot Noir grapes in North America were being grown. Ken preferred the fresh fruit profile of the Willamette Valley Pinot Noir. Though Wright wanted to move immediately, it would be several more years before he could afford it.

Finally, in 1986, he loaded his family, including then-wife Corby and their two young sons, Cody and Carson, into a moving van and headed toward McMinnville, towing along 10 barrels of Cabernet and Merlot produced from Martin Ray Vineyards in the Santa Cruz Mountains. This would be his first release of the Panther Creek label. Of course, the Bureau of Alcohol, Tobacco, and Firearms was on his case about the undocumented grapes, but somehow, after talking with Wright, they allowed him to sell the wine. It's hard to fathom how he managed to cut through that red tape, but he did. Though Panther Creek would soon become famous for Pinot Noir, the winery was actually launched with California Cabernet and Merlot.

Three years later, Corby and Ken divorced and in 1994, Panther Creek was sold to Ron and Linda Kaplan. In 1995, Ken married Karen Stecker, who was then a successful designer in McMinnville. They founded Ken Wright Cellars in a former glove factory in downtown Carlton and, in 1999, moved into a newly built winery. Today, the Wrights live on their Savoya

Pages 138–139: **The Savoya Vineyard was formerly a field for growing onions.**

Vineyard with their two daughters, Josie, 15, and Evy, 9, both adopted from Vietnam.

What Sits Beneath the Soil

In a video-recorded Powerpoint presentation Ken gave for *Wine Spectator*, he begins with a photograph of his wife, Karen, followed by a group shot of his wife and kids, then his extended family (including his "brilliant" grandson), then his second family (the staff at the winery), and a photo of his winery in Oregon. Then he takes a breath and backtracks some 200 million years to talk about one of his favorite subjects: mother rock, or the parent material, as he also calls it. "To understand Oregon is to understand geology," he tells the audience from his podium.

The topic also came up in our interview when we asked about his take on the quality of Oregon soil. "It's not the soil, the soil is unimportant," he said dismissively, much to our surprise. (In our other interviews, raising this topic always generated a lively discussion about Jory soil versus marine sediment, both hallmarks of Oregon geology.) "That's a misconception," he continued. "There are a lot of misconceptions in our industry. It's the parent material that counts. It's what sits *below* the soil that really matters. Soil is just a medium for the moisture the vines need, but what really makes a difference are the trace elements in the mother rock—potassium, manganese, phosphorus, calcium, copper, iron and such. It isn't until the roots are engaging parent material that you have the opportunity to see the real definition of wine and to really begin to get connected to that place."

A Blank Canvas

Wright pointed out to us that the Pinot grape is a blank canvas, unlike other grape varieties. "The inherent characteristic of Pinot is that it has no overriding trait," he explains. "Cabernet has an herbal quality; with Sauvignon you get a grassy element; and with so many varieties you get a trait that dominates place. Pinot Noir, though, is totally transparent, so everything you smell and taste is about place. That is what I find completely fascinating. To me, it is a great gift. It reminds us that we are not special. The best we can be is a fantastic steward of the property." Rather than stamp the wine with a varietal trademark, the Pinot grape provides the ultimate vehicle for conveying the

The winery is across the street from the tasting room.

aroma, flavor, and texture of the location in which it is grown.

Pinot Noir is also the most precocious red variety, ripening before any other. "It's wont is to ripen as fast as it can," explains Wright. "That's why it performs so poorly in warm climates—because it immediately reaches high sugar levels, forcing the farmer to harvest."

Yet, there are things that can be done to enhance the fruit on the vine, practices that promote vineyard health from mother rock to shoot tip. When planting, Wright pays particular attention to the site situation, new clonal and rootstock selection, and vine spacing and trellis systems, all of which are modified in each individual plot. This is pretty much standard at most vineyards, but Ken, unlike others, practices nutrition-based farming, and the story of how he came to understand and appreciate these sustainable methods is an interesting one indeed.

A $240 Melon

"The reality is, if you want to become a high-end, focused farmer, it's better to talk to people who are farming everything else," Wright says. "People who are farming hazelnuts, wheat, clover, grass seed." One such farmer is Norman McKibben from Walla Walla, Washington, a friend of Ken's from way back. One day Norman called Ken and advised him to come to Washington to see an orchard that was being farmed for the Japanese market.

The Japanese were demanding a different farming method compared to everything

Inside the tasting room, which sells jewelry by Karen Wright, among other items.

else that was growing in the area and following the advice of Dr. Arden B. Andersen, an agronomist, medical doctor, author, and one of the world's top consultants on advanced soil and crop management. Norman praised Dr. Andersen so highly that Ken decided to visit while Anderson was in attendance. He gathered five other Oregon farmers and headed to Walla Walla to meet the "Crop Doc."

"Anderson starts talking to us as he's peeling one of his apples," says Ken. "He sets the apple down on the counter and says we should go for a walk down the process line to see how gently they are handling the fruit. They have to be gentle because each piece of fruit has to be perfect. I don't know if you've been to Japan but in Tokyo, for example, the markets are unlike any other in the world. The fruits are displayed like jewels and the costs are insane. One melon can be $240."

This makes us gasp, trying to imagine who

would pay that kind of money for a melon. "Is it that they want it perfectly sphere shaped?" Nick asks.

Ken nods. "They want perfection because everything needs to have a perfect flavor. You get this by reaching what is called a complex carbohydrate state. When fruit is young, all the sugars in that fruit are simple sugars. Simple sugars easily oxidize. That's why when you peel an apple, it will start browning almost immediately. It's the sugars that are browning."

Linda asks, "So the apple Anderson peeled didn't turn brown?"

Ken holds up a hand and doesn't answer right away, telling us how they then took a tour of the plant and Anderson invited them to grab an apple off the line and taste it. "We did," says Ken. "We took a bite out of those apples and it was extraordinary. The amount of flavor, the depth of flavor, and the quality of the tissue was phenomenal. In a group of six of us, none had ever eaten such an amazing apple. We were all looking at each other and thinking this was unbelievable. Then, at the end of our tour, we went back to where Arden had greeted us and that peeled apple was sitting on the counter. It was pure, no browning, none. I looked at that and I thought, wait a minute. There's no way. There's no way.

"Andersen said, 'This is because we don't harvest early like most people do. Most harvest early and then think the apples will continue to mature. Well, they don't. Not in the same way at all. They need to be on the plant to properly mature.'"

Ken was so impressed that he arranged for Andersen to come to Oregon and consult with him and other growers. Over the years since then, Arden has returned about five times. "He spent a lot of time during his first visit going to every property and looking at the issues. It was amazing to learn from him, he taught us so much about nutrition."

Focused Farmer

Working with Andersen has changed the way Wright farms his vineyards. Each year, Wright will analyze the nutritional status of his soils and plants, take core samples to determine microbial procedures, and then tailor his methods to compensate for known deficiencies. No two vineyards have the same soil, so Ken will create a unique plan for each property.

While other winemakers we interviewed spoke about minimal intervention with the vines, Ken Wright was all about adding whatever was needed to spur the growth and help the plants. He talked a lot about microbiology, the process by which the plant breaks down raw ore into an ionic form that can be absorbed. "If you are a thoughtful and focused farmer," says Wright, "your greatest job is to ensure that there is an incredible population of microbiology where those roots meet the parent material." To this end, he is continually testing his plants' tissue and then feeding the plants what they need to achieve nutritional balance. The materials he uses to compensate for and replace nutritional deficiencies include manure, fish, and other additives. "But the single most important thing we add here in this region is lime, because we are so acidic. Nothing else is as important," he says, adding, "thank God lime is not that expensive."

Other grape growers talked to us about stressing the vines for maximum flavor, but this is not a practice Wright endorses. "Oh man, people say you have to stress the vines, but our hillsides are already stressed," he tells us. "If you are not focused on testing, testing, testing so that you can bring nutritional balance to the fruit, then shame on you. You'll get what you get and you won't know why."

In addition to nutrition-based farming, Ken Wright has been a leader in adapting and changing many of the traditional methods of winemaking in Oregon. In 1987, he introduced the idea of acreage contracts, whereby farmers are paid not by the weight of what they deliver but by the number of acres they farm. This helps provide some stability, so that farmers know how much money they will be earning for every acre planted. And it gives winemakers the freedom to take as much or as little of the crop as they want. Wright believes this system helped elevate the quality of the fruit grown in Oregon.

Gift of Nature

Ironically, while Ken constantly enhances the growth of his grapes, when it comes to making wine, well, he refers to that as "high-end babysitting." He tells us that the detail and expression of Pinot Noir wine comes from the vineyard, and that the role of the winemaker is to be completely transparent and not influence the flavor. "Our role is to farm in a way that we get a lot of expression and detail in the wines," he says, "and then provide great attention but no manipulation."

Though it is the tendency of human beings to tinker, this can have a negative effect in the cellar. According to Ken, "Certain things in this world are better left alone. Minimal handling of wine is essential to preserve what it is, a gift of nature."

Conferencing

Wright is proud of the fact that Oregon has never been afraid to be first at anything and cites the Steamboat Pinot Noir Conference as an example. The event is a gathering of all the Pinot Noir winemakers from around the world. The first meeting was in 1980 at the Steamboat Inn fishing lodge on the North Umpqua River near the famous Crater Lake and included winemakers from Italy, Burgundy, New Zealand, British Columbia, California, and Oregon.

The winemakers came to Oregon at the end of July with their wines, their concerns, and, we imagine, their fly-fishing gear. No press was allowed so everyone was able to talk freely and honestly about the issues they were facing. They could ask for help and get it. Now in its 36th year, the event has become very popular. "You almost need a lottery to get in." Ken laughs. "It's really cool that it happened first here in Oregon."

He also cites the International Pinot Noir Celebration (IPNC) as another Oregonian innovation. "It was the first real gathering to focus on single-varietal Pinot Noir. It was the first effort ever made by the industry to bring together all the foot soldiers to educate and entertain them while promoting our wines. We wanted the people in the stores who are selling the wines and the sommeliers who are recommending them, not the distributors. They come here, see our vineyards and taste our wines. They can hear our stories firsthand. We've been doing the event since 2000 and it's being copied everywhere because it's just a smart thing to do. Oregon has never been afraid to try something before everyone else."

Ken and Karen Wright believe in the spirit of volunteering and fostering a sense of community. Ken helped create an association of farmers who meet regularly and work to better the community.

For the town of Carlton, Ken's work with the Visioning Committee helped develop a 20-year plan for the area. He and Karen have been active in downtown improvements as well. They are also the founding members of two respected events in the valley: Carlton's Walk in the Park, an annual event that has raised more than $150,000 in support of local charities and service organizations; and ¡Salud!, a joint venture between the Oregon wine industry and Tuality Hospital, which provides health care for seasonal workers and their families. The Wrights also champion several projects benefiting young people and kids.

Communal Lunch

As our interview with Ken was winding down, he invited us to stay for the daily communal staff meal at the winery. We crossed the street from the tasting room and had a tour of the facilities. Then we pulled up chairs under the wisteria vines and joined the staff for a delicious homemade lunch of tuna tartare with giant vegetable chips and some amazing pie. It was obvious that the meal was just one of the numerous perks of working at Ken Wright Cellars. Many of the people we met had been there for a very long time and considered themselves part of the family. Ivory Duyn started at the winery when she was 14 and last year Ken officiated at her wedding. The cellar master, Alberto Alcazar, was working on

Ken Wright and Nick Wise, May 2016.

Ken and Karen Wright (far left) with their staff inside the winery.

the bottling line in 1997 when Ken promoted him. Vineyard manager Mark Gould was a chef in Portland when Ken offered him a job despite his lack of experience. "Ken always looks for people with great character," Karen recently told a reporter, "and then does whatever it takes to train them to do what needs to be done."

In the same way, he does whatever needs to be done to get it right in the vineyard. Wright's commitment to single-vineyard, site-specific winemaking shines through in every glass he pours. His wines are subtle and, with age, showcase the pronounced character of where

they came from. We don't know much about farming techniques or mother rock or many of the other things that Ken promotes, some of which are radically different from what other winemakers tell us. All we know is that the proof is in the tasting. Ken Wright Cellars is producing glorious wines with pinpoint flavors. One hundred of his wines have been awarded 90 points or higher by *Wine Spectator*.

He insists winemaking is not magic, that it's all based on science, analytics, and testing, testing, testing. Okay, Ken, we want to say, it may not be magic, but that is surely what it tastes like.

NICK'S TASTING NOTES

2014 Carter Vineyard Pinot Noir, Eola-Amity Hills

A more fruit-forward, juicy, and textured example of this cuvée than most years, the 2014 has retained plenty of structure to go the distance and improve with bottle age. All primary fruit flavors, the wine floods the mouth with ripe sinewy elements of black plum, raspberries, cherries, cranberries, heather, and flowers. Medium to full bodied for a Pinot Noir and lightly oaked, it coats the palate while carrying lithe, tangy acidity and powerful, sturdy, small tannins to the long finish. Expressive with a flavorsome, dark-laced fruity finish in the mouth, it will be interesting to see how this warmer vintage develops over time—should be great in 10 years. There were 781 cases made; 93 points awarded by *Wine Spectator*.

2013 Guadalupe Vineyard Pinot Noir, Eola-Amity Hills

Tangy and light in texture due to the nature of the bizarre vintage (Wright picked before the rains), this is a subtly complex wine on both nose and palate. Secondary aromas of graphite and mint cut a swath across the delicate raspberry and currant flavors. Long and earthy with a mosslike note that entwines the presently ethereal flavors. Good, but this wine needs time to integrate and mature; with a little patience it will show much more to come. Best to start drinking in 6 years. The winery produced 781 cases; 92 points were awarded by *Wine Spectator*.

2013 Freedom Hill Vineyard Pinot Noir, Willamette Valley

Plummy and spicy flavors were captured from the Freedom Hill Vineyard in this wine. Expansive in the mouth even though medium bodied with a firmer-than-usual structure, it still retains the brightness of red fruits and high acidity matched to some quite firm, sinewy tannins. The wine is quite lively, as it was a cool vintage; closed frame at the moment, it needs time to come together. There were 614 cases made; 89 points awarded by *Wine Spectator*.

2013 Savoya Vineyard Pinot Noir, Willamette Valley

The Savoya cuvée has always proved to be my favorite in Wright's portfolio (and not because of the onion trait!). This wine offers up wonderful nuances and layers of subtle secondary autumnal characteristics every time I get the chance to taste it, especially in the cooler vintages. The way it's developing proves it will age well. It's a mélange of exotic yet cool climate flavors and vegetal scents. Aromas of pine nuts and alpine flowers mingle with a distinctive and complex dried or hung meat note, making this wine a treat to the nose. Its mouthwatering acidity pairs with an expansive but delicate, savory palate and ends with ethereal minerals. This wine demands at least 5 years to develop and show its inner complexity. It was awarded 90 points by *Wine Spectator*.

KEN WRIGHT CELLARS

Tasting Room
120 N Pine Street
Carlton, Oregon 97111
503.852.7010
www.kenwrightcellars.com

Tasting Room: open Sunday through Thursday from 11am to 5pm, and Friday and Saturday from 11am to 6pm

ROCO

CHARDONNAY

Oregon • Vintage 2013

Chapter 9
At His Wits' End

ROCO WINERY

Newberg

Before arriving in Oregon, we had read and heard a lot about Rollin Soles, hailed in some magazines as the best winemaker in Oregon and known to many as the "Cowboy Philosopher." The nickname certainly fit on the morning we interviewed him at ROCO, his winery in the Dundee Hills, in late May 2016.

We arrived a little early and were seated outdoors with a big pot of coffee. Within a few minutes, Rollin came striding toward us. It didn't take a genius to guess he was from the West: the cowboy boots, handlebar mustache, and signature Stetson hat were dead giveaways.

We soon learned that though raised in Fort Worth, Texas, Rollin has lived in the Willamette Valley since 1986 and that he has loved Oregon for most his life. "This morning I got to play the Texan!" he tells us gleefully, explaining that he'd just come from a photo shoot with Véronique Drouhin (of Domaine Drouhin Oregon), where both winemakers were photographed on horseback for a French magazine cover. Not knowing exactly how to dress for the shoot, Rollin brought along his entire collection of cowboy hats and before our interview was over, all four of us were sporting Stetsons for a group photo. It was the start of

Rollin Soles—cowboy, philosopher, and winemaker—in his signature Stetson.

one of our most entertaining (and enlightening) interviews during our time in Oregon.

A Bunch of Happy Accidents

We wanted to know what inspired Rollin Soles, a Texas country boy, to become a winemaker, and were surprised to discover it happened in the hills of Switzerland, of all places. Soles had grown up around wine, having spent many years as a child in Jerez de la Frontera, Spain's sherry region, while his Navy aviator

ROCO Winery opened in the winter of 2012.

father was stationed in Rota. Later, Rollin earned a bachelor's degree in microbiology from Texas A&M, where his lifelong friendship with country singers Lyle Lovett and Robert Earl Keen began.

As an undergrad, Soles decided to spend a summer backpacking through Europe. When his biochemistry professor heard about those plans, he made Rollin a life-altering proposition. "He offered to get me a job with his wife's cousin, who turned out to be Hans Kesselring of Schlossgut Bachtobel, one of Switzerland's premier viticulturists," explains Rollin. "The vineyard was in the north of the country, where it's very steep and difficult to grow grapes. The guy turned out to be a huge inspiration to me. I ended up with so many friends and having so many fascinating conversations with these masterful Swiss winemakers. I found an abiding love of the culture of fine winemaking and fell in love with Pinot Noir while gazing at the Swiss Alps in the distance. It was a happy accident."

In fact, this is how Rollin repeatedly described the events in his life, as "a bunch of happy accidents." He is clearly one of those lucky individuals who recognized his calling early in life, which led him to discover the secret to happiness: "The first part of life is knowing what you want, the second part is figuring out where you want to do it, and the third is: don't mess it up!"

No wonder they call him the cowboy philosopher.

Not Messing Up

Returning home from Switzerland, Rollin applied to UC Davis to study enology and viticulture. "School was another happy accident," he says. "My roommate was from Oregon and we came up here to the Willamette Valley in 1979. The place just hit my heart. So by the time I was 21 years old, I had figured out what I wanted to do and where I wanted to do it. Happy accident!"

Yet, before he settled in Oregon, Soles was to travel the world learning his craft from the best mentors he could find. He worked at some top places, such as Wente Vineyards, in Livermore, California, and Chateau Montelena, in Napa Valley, and then traveled to South Australia to work at Petaluma Vineyards with founder Brian Croser.

Australia in the 1980s was a revelation to Soles, who had previously been totally focused on California. "I believed California was the center of the universe, but being in Australia really changed that perspective," he says. "I learned so much about viticulture and winemaking in Australia that I would never have learned in California." Many important English and Australian wine writers visited Petaluma, greatly influencing Rollin's youthful palate. Also, during his tenure Down Under, Bollinger Champagne invested in Petaluma, initiating Soles's first experience producing fine méthode Champenoise sparkling wines.

Rollin's talent was obvious from the very start and he did so well at Petaluma that Croser offered him the head winemaker's job in 1985. However, as much as Soles enjoyed winemaking in Australia, his heart was set on the verdant hills of Oregon. Willamette Valley was where he wanted to be but he saw an opportunity in Croser's job offer. Knowing his boss was looking to expand, Soles convinced him to check out Oregon as a possible new location. In 1987, they opened a winery in Dundee called Argyle.

Welcome to the Nuthouse

The place they purchased for Argyle was once a facility for drying hazelnuts. (Rollin was proud to point out that Oregon grows all of the hazelnuts for the American market.) "I like to say I took the nut-drying equipment out and left the nut—once a nuthouse, always a nuthouse," he says with an impish grin. Getting a sense of Rollin's wit, we began to understand why Argyle produces a "Nuthouse" vintage, with a label that originally sported a drawing of a squirrel.

In the mid-1980s, the demand for Oregon Pinot Noir was negligible, so Soles and Croser decided that Argyle would produce sparkling wine made from Pinot Noir and Chardonnay grapes that they purchased. They believed they could make consistent, high-quality sparkling wines, as the sugar requirement is significantly lower than it is for table wines. Their instinct was right. Ultimately, the Willamette Valley's climate proved to be ideal for growing wine grapes with ripe fruit flavors and the high acidity necessary for the best sparkling wines.

Eventually, Argyle would partner with Cal Knudsen (a founder of Knudsen-Erath and one of the original pioneers of Oregon winemaking), whose family vineyard became a prime source of fruit for Argyle. Knudsen would later invest in Argyle and serve as its chairman for 17 years. In 1996, Argyle purchased its first vineyard, Lone Star, the source for the winery's highly regarded Nuthouse wines.

While working at Argyle, Soles bought a 35-acre plot of land for himself in the Chehalem Mountains in 1987. "The farm really spoke to me," he says, "it was a very special place. I knew it was a magical plot for a vineyard and completely hidden in a cloistered spot. It's drop-dead gorgeous, on a gentle slope, with perfect soil and south-facing aspect." It would, however, be several years before he'd plant vineyards on his own property.

In 1999, he was divorced and a single dad to his daughter, Alexa, when he married Corby Stonebraker, previously the co-owner of Panther Creek Winery and former wife of Ken Wright. Born and raised in Chicago, Corby had earned a bachelor's degree in journalism from Arizona State University. She worked as an editor and writer in California and came to Oregon in the mid-1980s, contributing a strategic vision to the burgeoning wine industry. She was one of the founding members of the now famous International Pinot Noir Celebration (IPNC). She was also the mother of Cody and Carson Wright, when she and Rollin melded their two families into one big, happy, crazy-busy bunch.

At His Wits' End

Before ROCO, Soles produced Argyle's Nuthouse cuvées.

"The icing on the cake is that Corby and I got to start a business together," says Soles with

Left: **Rollin and Corby Soles.**
Below: **One of the many fanciful decorations
at ROCO doubles as a swing.**

genuine joy. The couple work together seamlessly with their complementary talents. "My wife meters my palate so that it's on target," Rollin explains, "and she has a great palate herself. When a couple work together, you want to divide up job titles and still have lines of communication. Corby is very, very good at understanding marketing and she loves the business side of the wine trade." Corby, who is a glass artist, also designed the winery's tasting room, adjacent to the winery, which opened in the winter of 2012.

Though Soles purchased his farm in 1987, because of family commitments and other obligations, it would be more than a decade before he planted any vines. As expected, he considers this delay another one of those happy accidents that have informed and enriched his life. In the 1990s, viticulture advanced rapidly in Oregon, with new clones and better growing methods, which he and Corby applied when they established their vineyard, now 20 acres.

They named the vineyard Wits' End. "The joke is that we live there, so that's where you often find us: at our Wits' End," explains Soles.

The Wild Essence of Their Wines

Wits' End was planted in 2001, the same year Argyle was sold to Australia's Lion Nathan, a food and beverage conglomerate. Soles remained Argyle's general manager and winemaker until resigning in 2013 to focus on the thriving ROCO Winery run by Corby. He remains in mentorship capacity with Argyle and other fine wine businesses of Lion and enjoys working with the young winemakers and growers.

Wits' End proved to be superbly located relative to the surrounding lands, just as Rollin knew it would. The Chehalem Mountains that rise up to the north behind the vineyards protect the vines from arctic winds in the winter; in the summer, the Dundee Hills to the south help to transition the Pacific Ocean winds into gentle afternoon breezes. Planted mainly in sedimentary soils among strands of native trees and two natural springs, the vineyard is a quintessential Willamette Valley landscape, teeming with wildlife—including owls, hawks, coyotes, and even cougars.

Because they are equal partners in every way, Rollin and Corby named their winery ROCO by combining the first two letters of their first names. For their label, they chose to use the striking symbolic imagery of rock

Argyle's thunderbird petroglyph logo.

petroglyphs from the Columbia Valley. The petroglyph is the Northwest's version of a thunderbird with other varieties found from Oregon up into British Columbia. Rollin and Corby believe the carved thunderbird captures the wild essence of their wine and embraces the history of the Pacific Northwest and ROCO wines.

The Stalker

ROCO's first release was in 2003, and the wines showcased a marked departure from Rollin's Argyle vintages. His stepson, Cody Wright, explains that the style at Argyle and ROCO are similar but the ROCO wines are more outside the box. "The Argyle wines were gorgeous and well built," Cody says, "but a little precise. That was Rollin's scientific side. At ROCO he is playing a little more." Indeed, at ROCO, Soles is free to experiment and he is certainly making wine his own way, often developing practices that are curious if not downright confounding to outsiders and other winemakers.

Most of the vineyards we visited in Oregon rely on dry farming, meaning the farmers depend on natural rainfall and do not irrigate their vines. They promote the idea of minimal intervention with the vines.

Soles has a different point of view, explaining to us that when vines are planted close together they are stressed already by competition, forcing the crowded vines to dig their roots deep into the rocks. "High-density planting creates so much competition for water that in drought years, a little water is imperative," he insists. "The most critical flavor-producing months in a vineyard are also the driest, and prudent irrigation ensures that wine grape flavors are encouraged and fresh tasting."

And then there is the story of The Stalker, which utilizes a winemaking technique Nick thought was the strangest one he'd ever heard of. "I always wanted to make wine that tastes of the vineyard, of fresh fruit," explains Soles. "With whole-cluster, the wines too often tasted green, vegetal, and stemmy. I could only taste the stalks."

In case you are not as fascinated with winemaking as we are, "whole cluster" means that after the grapes are picked, they are transferred into the fermenters with their stalks. Some winemakers think fresh stems add needed tannin and structure to the wine, while others disagree. (In Oregon, as elsewhere, there are as many opinions about the best way to make wine as there are vineyards.) "Whole cluster" is actually a very old-world method of winemaking, but today most winemakers de-stem their grapes because there are machines that can perform this chore with amazing speed and accuracy.

Anyway, back to Rollin, who once visited with Dario Boscaini, a producer of Amarone, a very rich Italian red wine made from air-dried grapes. (The word *Amarone* translates from the Italian as "the Great Bitter," just to give you an idea of the taste profile of this wine.) Soles realized that for Amarone, both the grapes *and* the stalks were air dried. He had a revelation. "Everyone focuses on the desiccated grapes and their concentrated flavor but not the stalks," he tells us. In 2011, he de-stemmed his grapes but instead of throwing the stems on the compost pile, he aged them for 7 to 10 days and, during fermentation of the grapes, added the stalks back into the mixture. He named the wine The Stalker. This wine is so labor intensive that he keeps the quantities to a minimum (around 600 cases) but says that the end result is worth the effort. "It's exciting to come up with a completely unique way to ferment red wine … that I believe no one has ever done," he explains.

Credit Where Credit is Due

Rollin Soles is a kind, humble, and generous man, which was obvious to us in the way he repeatedly credited people for helping him in his career. For example, he spoke very warmly about the Drouhin family, who came to the Willamette Valley around the same time as Rollin—in the late 1980s, when Argyle was founded. "This was the second wave of winemakers," says Rollins. "The first wave of pioneers proved you could make pretty good wine here—wine that attracted attention. Domaine Drouhin came in 1988 and the Valley would not have been the same without them. They understood the business of wine and brought both experience and capital. They also understood up-to-date enology and viticulture. We learned so much about viticulture from those guys, and they added credibility to Oregon winemaking."

He likes to emphasize the camaraderie he feels with his fellow winemakers, which is one of the aspects of the region that makes it so special to him. "What I've always admired about Oregon is that as grape growers and winemakers we tend to notice a problem and then solve it together," he tells us with the same pride he displays for all things Oregonian.

He is also enthusiastic about the young winemakers he has been able to mentor, especially his stepson, Cody Wright. "Oh man, I love that guy Cody," Rollin gushes. "He is fantastic. He's learned a lot from his dad, from me, and from his peers. He's determined to keep a different style, which I honor and think is really awesome. I never wanted to get in the way of his creativity or craft. It's really exciting to engage with young people and pass along our pioneer spirit for getting involved, being inclusive, and working together in the Willamette

Valley winegrowing community." He also champions Nate Klostermann, who was his assistant at Argyle and then took over as head winemaker when Soles left the Nuthouse for good. Speaking of Klostermann to the press, Soles said, "Nate has a great palate and he's calm under fire. He's going to be really good."

Pursuing the Grape

Rollin once told a reporter, "If the wine was made in the vineyard, as many claim, then there wouldn't be much reason for me to keep honing my craft. For me, great wine is the compilation of nature nurtured, and a personal vision and desire to finesse the juice to reveal its best. That's why I'm still pursuing the grape. Wine is a revelator."

When we asked about the future, he had only one word, "Chardonnay!" Soles has become the unofficial spokesperson for the promotion of Chardonnay in the Willamette Valley and is proud of the white wine he is producing at ROCO. "My joke is that my Chardonnay is the most un-American-style Chardonnay made in America," says Soles. "We capture the lovely, fresh, ripe pear, honeysuckle, and roasted hazelnut flavors, yet hold on to a mineral backbone that allows Chardonnay to transform itself with food." Indeed, we thought his Chardonnay was extraordinary—brilliant and graceful—a perfect reflection of its origin.

ROCO is also about to release a sparkling wine that we had the privilege of tasting, leaving no doubt that this ambitious new venture will also be a huge success. More accurately,

The 2013 RMS Brut (the initials stand for Rollin Michael Soles) is ROCO's first venture into sparkling wine and one of the best we've ever tasted.

it will just be the latest in a long line of successes for a winemaker who has been receiving somewhat unprecedented accolades over the past 20 years.

Rollin's wines have been named among the Top 100 Wines of the World by *Wine Spectator* 13 times, a distinction unmatched by any other Oregon winemaker. His very first ROCO vintage was poured in the White House. And in 2013, he was named one of the "20 Most Admired Winemakers in North America" by *Vineyard & Winery Management* magazine. Though still relatively small, ROCO is sold in 37 different states and 4 foreign countries; its success is a testament to the stellar reputation of the cowboy winemaker.

We wish we could end this chapter with a description of Rollin riding off into the sunset on his bronco, but alas, that is not what happened. Instead, he tipped his hat, jumped into his pickup truck, and scattered a cloud of dust as he drove off into the sunset. Close enough.

NICK'S TASTING NOTES

2015 RMS Brut, Willamette Valley

A phenomenal sparkling wine, one of the best I've ever tasted. Shows Oregon's potential for superb Chardonnay and Rollin's mastery of méthode Champenoise. Rollin's first attempt at making sparkling wine at ROCO (he mastered the art at Argyle) is a huge success! A blend of 67 percent Pinot Noir and 33 percent Chardonnay, the bouquet soars with stone fruits, nectarine, and citrus flavors, paired with light red fruits, all framed in creamy oak. The bubbles are persistent and the acidity formidable and high yet perfectly matched to the sweet, ripe fruit. The texture on the tongue is mouth filling, rich, and broad. Good tension between fruit and acidity leads to a creamy, satisfying, mineral-infused finish.

2014 Knudsen Vineyard Chardonnay, Dundee Hills

A tremendous wine with pinpoint balance between new- and old-world styles. Never ostentatious, this wine delivers the goods in a very understated but perfectly designed way, exuding a beautiful sense of effortlessness. The purity of fruit allows the terroir to shine through, and there's a great balance of fruit, acidity, and minerality. A gorgeous example of Soles's deftness with Chardonnay; light floral and spice oak accents add interest. Awarded 94 points by *Wine Spectator*.

2012 Knudsen Vineyard Pinot Noir, Dundee Hills

Produced on pure Jory soil, the light color and weight belies the power of this wine, which is brimming with cinnamon-accented bright cherry, dark black plum, blackberry, and cola flavors that persist on the long, expressive dried-spice/herbs, cola, and lightly vanilla infused palate. This wine earned 92 points in *Wine Spectator* and will be perfection with 6 more years' bottle age.

2012 The Stalker Pinot Noir, Willamette Valley

Made by aging the vines' stalks and then adding them back into the fermentation vessel (thus the name), there's no doubt this is a wine of quality, complexity, and structure, and begs for some additional bottle age to show its very best. The aged stalks add a more immediately palatable yet still formidable tannic structure, while the fruit is sleek, racy, and silky, exuding a mélange of vibrant, ripe black and red fruits, earthy spice, and minerals, with light notes of tree bark and savory aromatics that lead to a long finish. Best drunk in 10 years. Awarded 94 points by *Wine Spectator*.

2013 Wits' End Vineyard Pinot Noir, Chehalem Mountains

Fresh and focused, with scents of fresh cranberries and small *framboises* matched to floral notes, especially rose. However, look a little deeper for a dark core of mineral-laced blackberries and cassis fruit. Medium bodied, silky, succulent, and sleek, this wine is held together by bracing acidity and tight-grained, powerful tannins. It will age well and improve with a little extra bottle age. This vintage of Wits' End earned 93 points in *Wine Spectator*.

ROCO WINERY

13260 NE Red Hills Road
Newberg, Oregon 97132
503.538.7625
info@rocowinery.com
www.rocowinery.com

Tasting Room: open Thursday to Monday from 11am to 5pm

2013

VINTAGE BRUT

ARGYLE

GROWER ◆ SERIES

OREGON SPARKLING WINE
60% PINOT NOIR, 40% CHARDONNAY

Chapter 10

From the Nuthouse to the Haunted House and Beyond

ARGYLE WINERY

Dundee

We interviewed Argyle's winemaker Nate Klostermann on a bright and unusually non-rainy day in May. (We were even able to sit outside for a spectacular tasting.) Argyle was the ninth or tenth (it was hard to keep count) winery we visited on our extended tour of the Willamette Valley, so we had already become familiar with some of the more prominent names of the men and women (past and present) who had—and were—making history here. This was a bonus when we started talking about Argyle because so many of our previous contacts seemed to pop up as we discussed the evolution of this particular winery. Like many of the winemakers we met, Nate seemed to know all of the people we'd interviewed, either as working colleagues or close friends or both. We began to really comprehend that, here in Oregon, everyone's connected and there is no better example of that phenomenon than at Argyle.

To understand the evolution of Argyle, we need to backtrack a bit to some of our previous chapters on Erath and ROCO and introduce C. Calvert Knudsen, who planted one of Oregon's first and most important vineyards. Knudsen,

who died in 2009, was a Weyerhaeuser executive from Seattle in 1971 when he and his wife, Julia, bought a 200-acre former walnut orchard with two southeast-facing slopes in the Dundee Hills, which proved to be prime fertile land in the Willamette Valley. The following year, in partnership with Dick Erath, 30 acres were planted with grapes, making it the largest vineyard in the valley. Soon after, with

Winemaker Nate Klostermann outside the renovated winery.

Though the Knudsen vineyard surrounds the Erath Winery, the grapes are used for making Argyle wine.

60 acres planted, Knudsen became the largest vineyard in all of Oregon at the time.

In 1975, Cal and Dick formed the Knudsen Erath Winery partnership and received a permit to operate Oregon Bonded Winery No. 52 on the vineyard site; it was the first commercial winery in the Dundee Hills. For the next decade, Dick produced award-winning Knudsen Erath Winery wines. Cal, for his part, was a leader in quality innovations for the Willamette Valley and at the forefront of significant vineyard improvements in irrigation, clonal selection, planting higher vine densities, and conversion from own-rooted to root-stocked vines. The partnership between Dick and Cal ended in the late 1980s.

As we mentioned in the chapter on ROCO, Rollin Soles was working in Australia in the late 1980s and turned down an offer to become the winemaker at Brian Croser's Petaluma Winery because he wanted to fulfill his dream of moving to Oregon. Soles convinced Croser to look at expanding his operation into the Willamette Valley, which was around the same time as the breakup of Knudsen Erath. After purchasing a former nut-drying facility to start Argyle, Soles and Croser made a long-term grape-supplying agreement with Knudsen to use his fruit to make Pinot Noir, Chardonnay, and, most appealing to Knudsen, sparkling wine. "Producing sparkling wine was a great dream of my father's," reported Page Knudsen Cowles, Cal's daughter. "We pivoted all of our grape production [from Knudsen-Erath] to Argyle."

This explains why the Erath tasting room sits smack-dab in the middle of the Knudsen vineyard, whose grapes are used to make wine for Argyle. (Got it?)

To find Erath, you literally drive right through the Knudsen Vineyards; the conflicting signs have confounded many an Oregon tourist (including ourselves). The situation is more than confusing to Gary Horner, Erath's current winemaker, who lamented the fact that all those beautiful vineyards were growing right up to his very doorstep but were nonetheless unavailable to him.

With those very grapes, Argyle Winery has been producing world-class méthode Champenoise sparkling wine, Chardonnay, and Pinot Noir since 1987. In fact, Argyle was named Oregon's Premiere Winery in 2000 by *Wine Spectator* and its wines have been recognized 12 times in the magazine's list of "Top 100 Wines in the World."

In 2001, Argyle was bought by the spirits giant Lion when they acquired Petaluma, Brian Croser's Australian company, but the sale did not affect the quality or popularity of the Argyle brand. Rollin Soles remained as the winemaker and Knudsen Vineyard stayed the prime supplier of the highest-quality fruit to Argyle. Over the years, Argyle has won more awards for both still and sparkling wine than any other winery in Oregon.

The Knudsen vineyard remains family owned and is now operated by a second generation of Knudsens, Cal's four grown children—David, Page, Colin, and Cal Jr. Their father's legacy continues: in 2014 Knudsen released its first vintage in 25 years, under the stewardship of Nate Klostermann, which brings us back full circle to our interview with Nate and the utterly delicious 2011 Knudsen Vineyard Brut

we were drinking with him and Cathy Martin, Argyle's marketing coordinator, on that lovely day in May. "The Brut is our take on Blanc de Noirs out of Knudsen," Nate said as he poured. "It's high-elevation Dundee Hills with 90 percent Pinot, 10 percent Chardonnay." The interview could not have started on a tastier note.

Passing the Torch of Bubbles

In 2013, it was front-page news in all of the wine publications when Rollin Soles passed the torch to his former intern, and Nate Klostermann was appointed Argyle's head winemaker.

"I was lucky to have hired Nate," Rollin told a reporter that year. "He's turned out smarter than me with the usual skill sets of a fine wine palate, while being calm under stress—important when you need an understanding of both still wines and the complex sparkling wines that Argyle does so well."

At the time of his promotion, Klostermann was 31 years old, the same age as Rollin when he founded Argyle. Though still quite young, Nate is a very humble and grateful man. "I've grown up at Argyle and I am grateful for the rare opportunity to work alongside masters in their trade," Nate said in a magazine article about his appointment. "I have no intention of filling Rollin's shoes—that's impossible. Instead, I'll continue a lifelong journey of learning as we work together to honor the Argyle tradition. Living up to the standard we've already set is our top priority, but we're always trying to improve and learn the small techniques that make wine better. It's been a super-big learning period for me ... a huge bank of knowledge and wisdom that Rollin has passed down."

Shout Out to Innate Talent

Born in Wisconsin, Nate became interested in wine production while studying food science at the University of Minnesota. "I was thinking about doing brewing but in my last semester I took a course in wine science," Nate tells us. "They had an on-staff enologist and were trying to develop cold-hardy grapes that were halfway decent. So a lightbulb went off in my head. I wound up working for a small producer on the Mississippi River, down in Red Wing. By helping out in the vineyard and the tasting room, I got a feel for it. I thought I'd move out west and give it a try. A friend of mine put me in contact with Rollin and I started as an intern in 2005.

"I didn't have much wine experience when I got here," admits Nate, "but I had the most science experience of any of the other interns, so they threw me into the lab. I was mainly doing juice analysis, but I also did cellar work and tipping bins. It was a great combination of lab work and hands-on experience. Originally, I thought it would just be for harvest, but then they offered to let me stay on and it became full immersion into winemaking. I got lucky."

Luck may well have had something to do with it, but so did innate talent and mad skills. At Argyle, Klostermann was quickly promoted to enologist and then became Rollin's assistant, so his work was surely exemplary if it impressed Soles to such a degree. And, for Nate, it's hard to imagine a better mentor for anyone interested in winemaking. "I mean, 100 percent of everything I learned was from Rollin," Nate admits.

In 2008, Klostermann went to Australia to work with Brian Croser at Petaluma Winery, in Adelaide Hills, and Knappstein Enterprise Winery and Brewery, in Clare Valley, expanding his knowledge base. He returned to the Willamette Valley and has been at Argyle ever since. He works in collaboration with vineyard manager Allen Holstein and his staff, many of whom have been with the company for more than 20 years. Holstein, a very well regarded viticulturist from Kentucky, had been, in fact, working with Rollin Soles from the very beginning of Argyle.

We also just want to add as a side note that Allen Holstein, as mentioned in our chapter about Ken Wright Cellars, was Ken Wright's roommate when they were both in college. And Rollin Soles was one of Ken's teachers at UC Davis. (Remember our comment about how everyone is connected here!)

Nuts and Ghosts

When Brian Croser and Rollin Soles first came to the Willamette Valley, they purchased a facility in Dundee that had previously been used for

An engraved silver plaque commemorates Lena Elsie Imus, thought to be the benevolent spirit who haunted one of Argyle's buildings.

ARGYLE'S GHOST STORY

Built in 1883, our
Spirithouse story has
been one of reincarnation.

Oregon Pioneer, Lena Elsie Imus
lived and died here—her spirit still
walks the halls today.

These days, Lena is more of a muse,
welcoming you to a contemplative repose.

drying filberts. "Filberts are actually hazelnuts," Cathy Martin explains to us. "The Germans were calling them hazelnuts, so, to fit into the international market, Oregon decided to call them the same thing." Oregon grows something like 99 percent of all the hazelnuts in America and this facility used to be the main processing plants for distribution of the nuts around the world. In other words, it was a nuthouse. Soles delighted in this fact and decided to name The Nuthouse vintage after the winery's origins.

Adjacent to the nuthouse was a Victorian structure that became Argyle's tasting room and housed offices on the second floor. The house came with a legend all its own. Before Argyle, the building had served as Dundee's city hall, and according to many sources, it was haunted. The ghost was said to be the late Lena Elsie Imus, who used to live in the house and died in 1908, some say by her own hand, after she got pregnant and was abandoned by her lover. Though her spirit might live in Dundee, her actual remains are buried in Dundee's Pioneer Cemetery, next to her parents and brothers. Her tombstone is inscribed: *Not Dead, But Gone Before*, an epithet that is not only confusing and eerie, but also clearly inaccurate.

From the late 1970s through the 1980s, the ghost of Lena Elsie was said to cause strange occurrences in Dundee City Hall. Two people who worked in the building claimed to have frequently experienced inexplicable flowery scents, puffs of cold air, lights that would go on and off at random, and sounds of footsteps when no one was upstairs—in short, all the bump-in-the-night habits that ghosts traditionally exhibit when haunting the living.

Rollin Soles was more than amused by all the spooky speculation and admitted that people working at the winery had indeed reported some of the same strange occurrences. No one was really scared, though. (Soles himself claims that if the ghost exists, she is good spirited.) "I think it adds a great depth of fun and story to Dundee to have a ghost like that involved around here," Soles told a reporter. "It's a nice heritage piece." In tribute to the ghostly legend, Rollin named his Spirithouse vintage for her.

Bubbly

Argyle's main production is of still wines, even though they are best known for their sparkling wine, which have become increasingly beloved in Oregon. This is evidenced by the popularity of Argyle's tasting room, which seemed to always be packed, even when we visited in their off hours.

In the world of bubbly, Argyle is a rather small producer, but the quality and reputation of their sparkling wines have made them a significant player on the international market. Producing Brut, Blanc de Blancs, Brut Rose, and Extended Tirage Brut, Argyle rivals the long-heralded Champagne houses.

The grape varieties used in Argyle's sparkling wines are Chardonnay, Pinot Noir, and Pinot Meunier. Interestingly, Argyle sparkling wines are vintage-dated, meaning that all of the grapes used in a bottle are from the year printed on the label, which is not commonplace.

Argyle's 2005 Extended Tirage Brut.

at the higher elevations. Knudsen Vineyards is also the home of Argyle's Spirithouse Pinot Noir.

Since 1987, Argyle has expanded its growing capacity from Knudsen's original 120 acres by adding two other sites: Lone Star and Spirit Hill. Lone Star is located 15 miles south of Dundee in the Eola Hills. This 160-acre site was purchased in 1996 and is one of the warmest locations in Oregon. (Warm by Oregon standards that is!) Since 1999, Lone Star has served as the backbone for the Nuthouse Pinot Noir and, in 2005, Argyle released its first vintage of Lone Star-grown Riesling.

"The Willamette Valley has become such a highly regarded viticultural area due to our continuity and consistency in quality," says Nate. "Due to our cool-climate growing region, we also see true year-to-year vintage variations, which bring unique wines each year. Our sub-AVA growing regions also inform our style of winemaking, which emphasizes subtlety and nuance, while retaining structure for long-term ageability."

In 2007, Argyle purchased Spirit Hill Vineyard in the Eola-Amity Hills AVA, approximately 12 miles north of Salem. First planted in 2008, the vineyard is a total of 180 acres, making it now Argyle's largest vineyard, with 130 acres planted to Pinot Noir, Chardonnay, and Pinot Meunier—the varietals for Argyle's méthode Champenoise sparkling wines. The Spirit Hill vintage was launched to showcase the vineyard. In the northwest corner of this vineyard, tucked away among the towering ancient trees, is the old Pioneer Cemetery,

Many producers blend their sparkling wines with grapes from different years. This is called a non-vintage sparkling wine.

Argyle's vintage-dated wines are nothing short of spectacular. Their Extended Tirage Brut has been among *Wine Spectator*'s annual "100 Best Wines" four times since 2008, ranking between 17th and 25th.

The Vineyard Today

Argyle's Knudsen Vineyards Brut and their Blanc de Blancs originate from the historic Knudsen vineyards that feature old-world clones planted in high-density blocks on warm sites. The finest sparkling-wine fruit is grown

Argyle's 160-acre Lone Star Vineyard in the Eola Hills, purchased in 1996,
is one of the warmest locations in Oregon.

which inspired the name. It is also where Lena Elsie was laid to rest.

Under Construction

One thing we definitely noticed during our time in the Willamette Valley was all the construction going on at almost every turn. The main road into Dundee was being expanded and caused traffic to pile up every time we had to pass through the town. It was clear to us that this sleepy village was rapidly growing. Many of the wineries we visited had recently been built (ROCO and Chapter 24) or totally renovated (Ponzi and Adelsheim) or were currently under construction (Purple Hands) or in the planning stages for new architecture (Eyrie.) And among the most outstanding new designs we saw was Argyle, which had just completed a massive reconstruction in August 2015.

The upgrade was long overdue. After 28

years in the Nuthouse, Argyle had simply outgrown their physical environment. So, Argyle moved its winery from the Nuthouse in Dundee to a brand-new, much larger, facility in Newberg. (Argyle is the first winery within the city limits of Newberg, just as they were the first to open within the city limits of Dundee in the late 1980s.) At the time, Klostermann noted the reasons why they decided to expand into Newberg. "We like this site because of its consistency with our prior investments to promote sustainability, preservation of existing space, and limited impact on natural resources," he told a local reporter. The move meant that their available space for making wine went from 35,000 square feet to over 65,000, thus enabling Argyle to produce up to 120,000 cases annually.

The Nuthouse was then transformed into a much larger tasting room, which was essential to accommodate the tremendous numbers of visitors. Argyle, situated in a prime location right off Highway 99, has become a must-see destination for anyone on a wine tour of the Willamette Valley who loves the bubbly (include us in that category).

The contemporary design of the new tasting room is a marvel of imagination. Former crush pads below the high arches of the covered approach to the tasting room were converted to a place where visitors can sit and sip amid the native landscape. Sliding glass walls lead to an open, airy interior space that is functional and industrial yet surprisingly cozy and welcoming.

Inside the tasting room, native Douglas fir, discovered in the existing structure during

Above and pages 170–171: **The exterior of Argyle's exquisite new tasting room.**

More than 4,000 library wines are displayed in the tasting room.

half-full flutes and wineglasses. Nate had been extremely generous with his library wines, bringing out many of his favorite vintages for us to taste.

We thanked Nate for his time; he'd spent most of the afternoon with us and we worried that we were overstaying our welcome. "We don't want to keep you from your stuff," said Nick. "We know you are always busy."

"We really don't," Linda added, "but no way are we dumping this wine."

Nate laughed. "No," he agreed, "let's hang out and drink it."

Well, he certainly didn't have to offer twice.

demolition, was repurposed to make all the shelving, tables, paneling, and the extended bar. A climate-controlled room showcases more than 4,000 bottles of library wines while the entire line of wines available for purchase is artfully displayed. And the former Victorian house that was Dundee City Hall before it was Argyle's tasting room is now the new VIP meeting and event space for wine club members (and perhaps their ghosts as well.)

Hanging Out

As our interview with Nate wound down, the sun was setting over the horizon and the crowd in the tasting room began to disperse. It was very near to closing time but we didn't want to leave the beautiful setting and all the wonderful wines Nate had poured for us. Our table was overflowing with opened bottles and

Hanging out with Nate Klostermann.

NICK'S TASTING NOTES

2011 Knudsen Vineyard Brut, Dundee Hills

This sparkling wine is youthful, light, fresh, and very hightoned, with expressive aromas of pears, green apples, and citrus fruits, and a floral and sea salt overlay. Pure, precise, grassy, and light bodied, it has an elegant crystal-like sheen. Persistent effervescence, light autolytic notes, and laserlike acidity bring this wine to a chalky, mineral-laced lengthy finish. Drink now. There were 906 cases made; awarded 91 points by *Wine Spectator*.

2011 Knudsen Vineyard Blanc de Blancs Sparkling Wine, Dundee Hills

This Jory soil vineyard planted in 1974 is amusingly situated at the Erath Winery. A light gold color with small, tight persistent bubbles introduces this wine to the drinker. Fresh, zippy, and bready aromas leap from the still tight autolytic nose. Precise, pure aromas of red currants, cut limes, fresh hay, minerals, and a light aged note of cashew nuts and cream fill the mouth. This medium-bodied wine reveals deep cool-climate flavors and a red-berry note. Received 91 points from *Wine Spectator*.

2012 Blanc de Blancs, Dundee Hills

Situated at a high elevation of 850 feet, Julia Lee's single block provides the grapes for this always elegant, creamy textured and toned wine. 2012 was a warm vintage and the wine benefited from the extra heat, adding a touch less austerity than usual. The color is youthful and shiny with a green tinge; the bubbles are persistent and small. In the mouth the wine immediately opens up broadly; it is long, clean, and fresh with vanilla-tinged aromas of citrus, pear, and Granny Smith apple. Bready autolytic notes fill out the impressive mid-palate.

2005 Extended Tirage Brut, Willamette Valley

Elegant, refined, concentrated, and complex, this is a knockout example of a sparkling wine. This excellent cuvée utilizes two-thirds Pinot Noir and one-third Chardonnay in the blend and is then aged for 10 years in bottle before it's disgorged and released. The wine thus retains an amazingly fresh, vibrant character and presents with a medium deep gold color and very fine bubbles. Aged, nutty, bready aromas are dispersed with medium-bodied but broad and very concentrated notes of citrus and pear, accented by just emerging secondary notes of spice, white chocolate, white truffle, brioche, coffee beans, and cream, lifted by high bracing acidity. Lithe, generous, and textured, this wine is extremely long and delicious. There were 1,012 cases produced; awarded 93 points by *Wine Spectator*.

2015 Reserve Pinot Noir, Willamette Valley

This still wine is comprised of grapes from all three of the estate's vineyards and presents juicy aromas of red sweet fruits and a wonderful silky texture in the mouth, exuding concentrated layers of crisp red summer fruits plus a long vanilla spice-infused finish. Good minerality, a tight, sweet tannic frame, and racy acidity ensure the wine's future complex bottle development. I love Argyle's still wines as they are immediately drinkable but also have exquisite balance to take the test of time. Received 91 points in *Wine Spectator*; 975 cases were produced.

1999 Nuthouse Chardonnay, Willamette Valley

It's absolutely astounding how this library bottle of Chardonnay has retained its freshness, fruit concentration, and balance. It's savory but still wonderfully balanced and soft, with generous levels of oaked citrus fruits held aloft by the high acidity. Rich, ripe, and concentrated, with amazing integration of all components on the palate, this is a very complete wine with a long extemporary finish. Awarded 91 points by *Wine Spectator*; 1,200 cases were produced.

1999 Nuthouse Pinot Noir, Willamette Valley

Using selected prime lots of Pinot Noir from their various vineyards, Argyle's reserve wine ages superbly but can also be enjoyed on release. The expressive bouquet includes aromas of aged, dusty, super-ripe black cherries, cassis, and plum fruit that mingle with fresher, more sprightly red fruit characteristics. Tertiary notes of damp earth, licorice, meat juices, and floral and spicy scents lurk and pop out from the background, and thus the wine retains continual interest. Medium bodied but generous, rich, soft, and broad, with integrated tannins and high acidity. Received 93 points in *Wine Spectator*.

ARGYLE WINERY

691 Highway 99 W
Dundee, Oregon 97115
503.538.8520
tastingroom@argylewinery.com
www.argylewinery.com

Argyle Tasting House: open daily from 11am to 5pm; for parties of 10 or more, call for details and options

CRISTOM

Eola-Amity Hills
Willamette Valley

Pinot Gris
Estate
2014

PRODUCED AND BOTTLED BY CRISTOM VINEYARDS, INC., SALEM, OR
ALCOHOL 14.0% BY VOL.   PRODUCT OF THE U.S.A.

Chapter 11

A Little Touch of Corruption

CRISTOM VINEYARDS

Salem

Cristom Vineyards is well known for producing benchmark Pinot Noir wines that today are sold in more than 40 states and 16 countries, including England, where Nick first came across the label, tucked away on a shelf at his local wine shop, Handford's, in West London. This was one of Nick's early introductions to Oregon Pinots, and the bottle sparked his interest in the region. Here was a wine that could compete with the best of his favorites from Burgundy.

The Cristom vineyard itself is beyond beautiful, planted with glorious flowers that were in full bloom when we arrived on a rainy afternoon in late March. But the real highlight of our visit was due in no small measure to the charms and passions of winemaker Steve Doerner, who met us at the tasting room and then proceeded to host a remarkable three-hour barrel tasting covering some 17 vintages. He was a most gregarious host, knowledgeable in all aspects of winemaking, especially in Oregon, and a downright unpretentious fellow with a wonderful sense of humor.

An Exceptional Pinot Noir

Established in 1992, Cristom was inspired by

The entrance to Cristom on a rainy day in March 2016.

a particular bottle of wine that ignited the passion of Paul Gerrie. A lifelong wine lover, Paul recalls his first taste of that exceptional Pinot Noir: "It was a 1980 Échezeaux and it was astonishing. From that point on, I was hooked on Pinot!" We would hear a similar version of this story many times during our travels: a brilliant bottle of Pinot Noir giving rise to a new appreciation of wine and, ultimately, a career in winemaking.

Steve Doerner, Mark Feltz, and Tom Gerrie.

In the 1980s, Paul, his wife, Eileen, and their two young children were living in Pennsylvania. Paul, an oil engineer who'd done very well in the business world, was looking for a new challenge. In 1991, the Gerries attended the International Pinot Noir Celebration (IPNC) in McMinnville, Oregon, and fell in love with the area. Like many people who discover Oregon with an open heart, the Gerries were soon thinking about a life-altering move.

Unsure of exactly where in Oregon to buy land, Paul turned to Mike Etzel (from Beaux Frères) for advice and guidance. Together, they looked at three or four listings before settling on a property about 10 miles north of Salem and 10 miles south of Dundee. One year later, the Gerries left Pennsylvania, moved to Oregon, and christened the vineyard by combining the names of their two kids, Christine and Tom.

It took a bit of imagination to see the potential of their new property, as it had lain abandoned for about four years. Huge swaths had to be torn out, but ultimately the land would prove to be uniquely ideal for growing grapes. With marine sediment at the bottom and volcanic soil at the top, the earth here is a layer cake of fertile soil and sediment.

In another aspect of setting up his vineyard—namely hiring personnel—Paul Gerrie was either extremely prescient or just plain lucky. At the winery's inception, he brought in vineyard manager Mark Feltz and winemaker Steve Doerner, who are now also part owners in the operation.

By 2012, Paul was ready to retire, and Tom Gerrie took over from his father.

"We started as a 2,500-case producer," explains Tom, "with about 1,500 cases being Pinot Noir. Today, Cristom produces between 15,000 and 16,000 cases a year."

A Family of Winemakers

Mark Feltz grew up in a winemaking family. His father, Jim Feltz, planted the Feltz Vineyard in 1973. "He was a bit of visionary," explains Mark. "Feltz Vineyard was one of the first in the Eola Hills, an area that's now home to more than 2,000 acres of grapevines. As a kid, I worked digging holes and putting vines into the ground. Later, in the early 1980s, I worked with Ted and Terry Casteel at Bethel Heights [Vineyard]." Mark also worked at Stag's Leap, in Napa, and Chalk Hill, in Sonoma, but his heart was always in Oregon. "I was looking for an opportunity to get back into the vineyard when I got a call from the Casteels, who had just met with Paul Gerrie," says Mark. "Paul was searching for someone to manage

his vineyards. I leapt at the chance to return to viticulture and my Oregon roots. I've worked at Cristom since the first harvest and I love it."

While some winemakers are born into the profession and learn to appreciate the art at a young age, others come to it on their own, which was what happened to Steve Doerner. His entrance into winemaking was more in the realm of being a lucky coincidence. Asked how he got started, he replies, with a shrug, "I was

Above: **Tom Gerrie at the fermentation tank.**
Pages 180–181: **Aerial view of Cristom Vineyards.**

"Wine guardian" Steve Doerner with author Nick Wise.

left on the sideboard and if it was still around after a week, it was probably okay because of all the preservatives."

In the late 1970s, Doerner was a student at UC Davis, which boasts an exceptional viticulture program, but he was studying biochemistry. "Actually, I was there for pre-med," explains Steve, "but soon realized I wasn't going to cut it. One day I asked one of my professors if wineries ever hired biochemists. He said not to his knowledge. But a month later, he got a letter from Josh Jensen at Calera asking specifically for biochemists and microbiologists, and my professor alerted me. The rest is history. I spent 14 years learning how to make wine at Calera."

It is unlikely that Steve, or any young wine enthusiast, could have found a better teacher than Josh Jensen, who at that time was one of the most famous winemakers in California and one of the first to bring Pinot Noir to the region. Jensen also proved to be a very generous employer, arranging for Steve to travel to Burgundy and, through his contacts, meet with such great French winemakers as Jacques Seysses, at Domaine Dujac; Aubert de Villaine, at Domaine de la Romanée-Conti; Jean-Marie and Christophe Roumier; and Hubert De Montille. These winemakers would greatly influence the young biochemist. Indeed, of all the winemakers we met in Oregon, Doerner was, undoubtedly, the most Burgundian— both in his attitude and in the old-world style of wine he produces. Doerner's wines have the rustic, authentic, traditional taste of what we associate with French heritage winemaking.

at the right place at the right time." Certainly, his appreciation of good wine did not come from his family, even though his grandparents were from France and he still has distant cousins there. "I think part of how I got into winemaking was curiosity about my French heritage. I wasn't a total novice, I grew up having wine around the house," he admits, "but it wasn't good wine. It would be a gallon jug

A Little Touch of Corruption

We asked if Steve thought Cristom's wines were more in the style of Côtes de Beaune (meaning light and red fruity) or more Côtes de Nuits (dark and lush). We consider the first to be the more feminine and the other more masculine, or as Nick likes to say, "If in Bordeaux, one would be the Left Bank and the other, the Right Bank."

Doerner mulled the question over and replied, "It's hard for me to say, but our wines are certainly more European than new-world wines, and that's what I am most proud of. Too many people come to this 'bigger is better' philosophy and their wines are ultra-sanitized and filtered. I think you take a lot of personality out of wine when you handle it, so I try not to."

Cristom's basic philosophy of nonintervention seems simple enough. "The industry has been around for six to ten thousand years, so winemaking to me is not brain surgery," Steve says with his signature humility. "It is not hard; anyone can do it. You have to have good starter material and then not screw it up."

To us, Steve represents a kind of fly-by-the-seat-of-your-pants style of winemaking. Most winemakers like to be in total control, or at least think they are, but Doerner likes to let nature take its course; only interfering when it is deemed absolutely imperative. For example, many Pinot Noir winemakers are now doing what is called a "cold soak," which is when the grapes are brought inside right after picking, cooled, and left to soak in water for five to six days. Invented in France by Henri Jayer, this process is meant to add pigmentation and flavor, without extracting tannin, and cool down grapes grown in warmer climates to stall fermentation. Yet Doerner scoffs at such interventions. "Usually when I find something new or trendy, I wind up not liking it because I'm more of a traditionalist," he admits. "Virtually everyone in the valley is now doing a cold soak—and even in Burgundy, too—but I don't find it to be beneficial. I'm not filtering the wine, either. I don't want any brett [bad yeast] in the wine if I can avoid it, but I am not doing anything in particular to stop it. Hey, no one wants stinky, rotten wine, but I find that sometimes a little touch of corruption can be interesting."

His point seems to be that when wines are made "too correctly," they are missing some of the flaws that Doerner finds appealing. By-the-numbers winemaking is definitely not in his playbook. Neither is a strict adherence to rules and regulations. We particularly enjoyed Doerner's laidback attitude in his cellar. Asked why certain barrels were placed in a corner, he shrugged and said, "No other place to put them." And after we'd tasted his offerings from the barrel, he poured the excess from our glasses back into the barrel; something we'd only ever seen done before in France.

Land vs. Hand

For years, there's been a "land vs. hand" debate in the wine business. Which is more important: the terroir or the person making the wine? This reminds us of something Robert Kamen (of Kamen Wines, in Sonoma) told us when we interviewed him for our first book. "You can make bad wine from good grapes," he said, "but you can't make good wine from bad grapes."

True enough, but in the end, which is more important: the winemaker or the vineyard? Doerner thinks you can't separate the two; both are critical. And he believes that there's another factor to consider. "You have to include the vintage in the equation," he insists. "Vintage can beat everything. Take our 2003 vintage, for example. That was a baking hot year and you could not make an elegant wine no matter what you tried. You could pick early but the fruit would have been underripe and simultaneously dehydrated. We chose to wait for flavor but had to add water to some fermenters or we would've ended up selling jam. Here was a perfect example of vintage trumping both terroir and winemaking."

Wine Guardian

We soon learned that Doerner is not so big on percentages. When asked, he could not tell us the amount of new oak in his barrels, saying he leaves the art of barrelmaking to the coopers. He buys from 12 different coopers and expects all of them to provide him with their best pieces. He berates the fact that most winemakers want total consistency in their barrels.

In the tank with Steve Doerner and Tom Gerrie.

Under the fermentation tank with Tom Gerrie and Steve Doerner.

Getting all the barrels to be exactly the same, Steve explains, is literally impossible. "I want to tell them [other winemakers], a tree is a living thing; Mother Nature does not give the same fruit every year, so why should the barrels have to be the same every year? Naturally, you want to rely on the cooper for some consistency, but it's nature; it's a continuum."

While some winemakers favor heavy toasts and others prefer an almost neutral barrel, Steve sees the advantage in both. "I like diversity," he says, which comes as no surprise to us.

We also discovered that Doerner doesn't like labels. Even the title "winemaker" irks him. He prefers the French word *vigneron*, which literally means "the person who takes care of the vines." And this is how Doerner sees his role in the process of winemaking.

"In France, you make the wine in the vineyard," he says, "and you leave it alone as much as you can. I used to say I do 'nothing,' but then along came the 'natural wine movement' and they *literally* do nothing, so I had to change that statement. I just want to make a wine that's balanced and do whatever to accomplish that, but I am very hands off."

It seems to bother him that here in America, everyone has to have a title. "It's weird," he says, "I'd rather have no title, or if I had to have one, I'd use the term *wine guardian*." Whatever he calls himself, Steve Doerner is a true original. And Cristom's wines are perfect examples of rugged determination and a noninterventionist attitude. Though Steve chooses not to have complete control, in the end, Cristom's wines have an enviable consistency. Steve and Tom know exactly what they're doing, or perhaps it's more accurate to say "not doing." Either way, we think Cristom Vineyards is very fortunate to be under their stewardship.

NICK'S TASTING NOTES

2012 Sommers Reserve Pinot Noir, Willamette Valley

This cuvée displays a translucent dark ruby color; the nose is swathed in the aromas of red forest fruit—ripe raspberries and cherries—and damp earth, flora, chocolate, and an aged, spicy, savory note all pair with red loam, iron, and mineral scents. A black streak of cassis fruit runs down the core or mid-palate. High but very balanced acidity and decent sweet tannins provide further aging capacity over the next 6 to 7 years. A nice, long, expressive floral flourish lingers at the back end.

2012 Marjorie Vineyard Pinot Noir, Eola–Amity Hills

One of our favorite cuvées in Cristom's vast portfolio, this wine typifies the estate. It abounds with flavors of fresh raspberries, red cherries, and loganberries when young; however, as is true in many of the estate's Pinots, a liquorlike ripe streak of black fruit runs through its core, adding wonderful mid-palate sweetness with extended bottle age. The texture is plush and inviting; the wine has an excellent depth of sweet fruit and the finish is long, exhibiting a fine tannic framework. Just beginning to hit its stride, this wine will be superb in 4 to 6 years and will last 20 more, yet is beautifully drinkable now. It was awarded 93 points by *Wine Spectator*, and only 213 cases were produced.

2002 Marjorie Vineyard Pinot Noir, Willamette Valley

This wonderfully ancient cuvée of "Marjorie" demonstrates Cristom's aging ability. The warm vintage produced a fleshy wine with good aging potential due to the thick skins on the grapes. It's very savory at present but has a beautiful depth of red and black fruits that join haunting notes of violet, meat juices, tapenade, orange rind, and Marion berries. Fruit, tannin, and acid seem to have melded perfectly. High acidity, but as with all the Cristom cuvées not at all eye flittering, just deftly balanced and supportive. With excellent texture and a superb finish, this wine can age another 5 to 6 years but is delicious now.

2012 Jessie Vineyard Pinot Noir, Eola-Amity Hills

Produced from the east-facing Jessie Vineyard, this cuvée shows much more of a dense black-fruit character and a richer, firmer overall structure and texture than the Marjorie. Medium bodied with supportive acidity, the palate is a mélange of black and red summer fruit flavors accented with floral and mineral notes sitting on a chewy tannic frame. This wine is still youthful but delicious and has a very long finish, indicative of its quality and ageability. Give it another 5 to 8 years for best results.

2013 Estate Syrah, Eola-Amity Hills

Strange to come across a Syrah in Pinot country, but Cristom does a great job with this very sleek, clean, ripe black-fruited wine. It has plenty of bold concentrated fruitiness, good tannic sweetness, and proper varietal Syrah spiciness sitting on a medium-bodied frame. It's textured and long on the tongue, powerfully flavored with white spice, fresh bread, meat, and tar, plus of course the requisite uplifting acidity of the region. Only 188 cases were made.

CRISTOM VINEYARDS
6905 Spring Valley Road NW
Salem, Oregon 97304
503.375.3068
www.cristomvineyards.com

Tasting Room: open Tuesday to Sunday from 11am to 5pm

Archery Summit

Dundee Hills Pinot Noir

2005

ARCHERY SUMMIT ESTATE

750 ml ALC. 14.0% BY VOL.

Chapter 12

Cave Dwellers

ARCHERY SUMMIT

Dayton

Above: **Aerial view of Archery Summit Winery.**
Pages 190–191: **Entrance to the lounge in the underground tasting room.**

The windy drive up to this winery follows Archery Summit Road (after which the winery was named). From the outside, the building looks like many wineries in Oregon. Sand-colored brick covers a low-slung, somewhat French chateau-style building, giving off an air of sophistication. In the parking lot, signs point out that the tasting room is toward the right. A path leads to a long, dark corridor and

a massive glass door that opens with a quiet swoosh into the most unique private tasting room in the Willamette Valley, a jaw-dropping manmade cave.

The walls and low ceiling are composed of broken rock that was blasted out of the mountainside in the early 1990s. It took two years to dig what would ultimately be a quarter mile of caves that serve as Archery Summit's

underground barrel room. The temperature in the caves is cool and the ambiance is soothingly quiet and serene. (If you want to know what it's like to visit the subterranean cellars of Burgundy's Côte d'Or and get a feel for how they make wine in the South of France, come visit this tasting room.)

Drilling these caves while constructing Archery Summit's five-level gravity-flow winery was a huge undertaking that took a lot of imagination, perseverance, and confidence. However, once we learned more about founder Robert "Gary" Andrus, we came to understand how such a truly daunting task could be both conceived and executed.

A Flamboyant Winemaker

Unlike the early pioneers that we've profiled in this book, Andrus was not one of those

At the winery's entrance on Archery Summit road.

winemakers who discovered a fabulous Pinot Noir or Burgundy that turned around the direction of his life. No, Andrus was too busy skiing and trout fishing. He started making wine at a later age, having had quite an exciting and diverse career before he became interested in wine.

Born in 1946, Andrus grew up in Arcadia, California, where he developed a passion for skiing. He studied political science at Brigham Young University, became captain of the ski team, and was ranked third in the nation on the US ski team. After obtaining an MBA at Oregon State University, he started a sporting-goods chain of stores in central California, which he then sold in 1975 to embrace his love of the outdoors as the vice president of a Colorado ski resort. In 1978, he decided to pursue another passion and moved to Napa. He and his second wife, Nancy, started Pine Ridge Winery (which also boasts a 34,000-square-foot manmade cave dug deep into the hillside).

Over the next two decades, the couple greatly expanded Pine Ridge, while Gary mastered his winemaking skills in the Bordeaux varietals of Cabernet Sauvignon, Merlot, and Malbec, and the white varietals of Chardonnay and Chenin Blanc. He was a leader in the move to stress the importance of appellations in America, especially the Stags Leap District AVA, where Pine Ridge is located. In 1993, Gary set his sights on the Willamette Valley, in partnership with Ian Cumming of the Crimson Wine Group. "At the time it was very visionary to go to the Dundee Hills (from California) to establish a benchmark Pinot Noir producer," says Patrick DeLong, who was promoted to CEO of the Crimson Wine Group in 2015.

Andrus and his partner purchased two vineyards—Arcus and Red Hills—and began excavating the hillside. That year the grapes from those vineyards were trucked back to Pine Ridge to make an introductory vintage for Archery Summit. In 1995, Archery Summit released its first vintage made from grapes grown in Oregon.

Raising the Bar for Pinot

Though Andrus may have come a bit later to Oregon (two decades after the first wave of winemakers), his arrival made a huge impact in the Willamette Valley. He made head-lines in the mid-1990s when he released his Pinot Noir at the unheard-of price of $50 a bottle. Up to that point, no one in Oregon had dared retail their relatively unknown wines for more than $25 a bottle. Perhaps it took an outsider from Napa to see that customers would pay a premium price for a premium wine that was ranked among the very best in the state. His groundbreaking decision helped alter the perception of the value of Oregon Pinot Noir.

Andrus was famous for his unique growing and winemaking techniques, which allowed him to ripen his grapes two weeks earlier than normal, long before the autumn rains arrived to disturb the crops. And he was a mentor to many young winemakers, including Josh Bergström of Bergström Wines. Gary once sold

Archery Summit Pinot Noir meets our first book.

a few tons of grapes from his prized vineyard to Bergström even though it detracted from Archery Summit's production. "Gary was a very complex personality," Bergström admits, "a bon vivant and a driven winemaker and businessman."

By 2002, Gary was divorced from his second wife, Nancy, and he sold his Pine Ridge and Archery Summit shares to the Crimson Wine Group, which also owns Seghesio Family Vineyards, in Sonoma, and Chamisal Vineyards, in San Luis Obispo. In 2004, Gary remarried and, with his new wife, Christine, started Gypsy Dancer Estates in Oregon; they also purchased a Pinot Noir property in New Zealand. Combining the two estates might've made for a brilliant new venture, but Andrus did not live long enough to find out. He died in 2009, at the too-young age of 63.

"I know that I would not be making Pinot Noirs at the level we are today without the influence of Gary Andrus," Josh Bergström told a reporter after Andrus's death. "Gary brought a certain professionalism, competitive drive, and price point to Oregon. When Archery Summit showed up in Oregon, we had never seen the likes of Gary, and I doubt we ever will again."

Legacy

Andrus's legacy at Archery Summit survives him. The winery he pioneered features a gravity-flow system for winemaking, decreasing the need for mechanical pumps to transport must and wine among fermenters, tanks, and barrels. The design utilizes five levels: grapes received at the crush pad on the topmost level travel downward, one floor at a time, to the fermentation hall, aging caves, and bottling area.

The fermentation hall at Archery Summit.

By using an elevator built into the cellar 60 feet below ground, barrels can be lifted for racking and blending and filled without the use of pumps. This process prevents any stress on the wine that might impair its essence. Likewise, the winemaking team employs special fermentation techniques and varies barrel regimen to precisely match the cooper and toast level with the specific vineyard blocks and vintage conditions. These extra efforts allow Archery Summit to craft wines that vividly express their distinct terroir, or place of origin.

Small, temperature-controlled fermentation tanks are combined with native yeast fermentation. The Pinot Noirs are aged for up to 18 months in the underground caves, where more than 550 French barrels are maintained at a constant temperature, from 55°F to 59°F, throughout the year, with a humidity level below 75 percent. These are optimal conditions for storing wines maturing in barrel. (Visitors can explore the underground cellar with a tour of the winery and discover firsthand how the architecture is critical to the production of the wines.)

Archery Summit has just over 115 acres and six estate vineyards: Archery Summit Estate, Red Hills Estate, Renegade Ridge Estate, Looney Vineyard (Ribbon Ridge AVA), Archer's Edge, and Arcus Estate. The vineyards are planted primarily in prime Jory soil in the Red Hills of Dundee. The plantings are dense, vertically trellised, and sustainably farmed. All the Pinot Noirs (except the Premier Cuvée, the winery's signature blend) are vineyard designated (produced from a single vineyard).

More than 550 barrels are stored in the massive underground cellar.

Today, the winery produces 14,000 cases annually, the majority of which are sold directly to consumers through the wine club and tasting room.

Speaking of Caves

We took a tour of the amazing caves at Archery Summit before our scheduled interview. And speaking of caves, we want to give a shout out to the Oregon Caves National Monument and Preserve, which is about 300 miles south of the Willamette Valley (far away, we know, but well worth the trip). Nestled deep inside the Siskiyou Mountains, the caves were discovered in 1874 and have been a tourist attraction ever since. Known as the Marble Halls of Oregon, the caves were formed out of marble as rainwater from the ancient forest above dissolved the stone. Tours are offered from mid-April through early November. As a bonus, those marble caves lead to the mind-boggling Crater Lake, one of the so-called Seven Wonders of Oregon and an absolute must-see. Yes, this is

The private tasting room in the underground cellar.

a bit off-topic, but it's hard to talk about the state of Oregon without mentioning at least one of its many natural wonders—aside from the wine, that is.

Back at Archery Summit's manmade caves, we sat down to an extended interview with winemaker and general manager Chris Mazepink, whose delightful and unique last name matched his winning personality. Chris was very generous with his time and wine and extremely knowledgeable about Oregon winemaking.

We were still marveling at the cave setting when Chris pointed to the walls and told us that the deepest recorded vine roots in the Willamette Valley are about 75 feet below the surface. "The barrel and tasting room are 42 feet below the surface of the Archery Summit Estate-Vineyard," said Chris, "but it was Gary's vision to eventually have the vine roots come down into the tasting room and cellars, through the roof, just like in Champagne."

Mazepink

Chris Mazepink's journey to become a winemaker took some quirky twists and turns. In college, he majored in cultural anthropology, business management, and theology, which allowed him to study abroad for half of each year. He spent a semester at the University of the West Indies in Kingston, Jamaica, as well as some time in Cape Town, South Africa, Guatemala, Chile, and Belize. None of these journeys involved wine, but then he got a job working in a wine shop and began trying wines from around the world. "Each night I'd take a bottle from some famous winemaking area of the world and taste it," he says and then laughs. "On payday, I'd end up owing the store more then they owed me—but I was okay with that." Call it the cost of his wine education.

Winemaker Chris Mazepink.

As graduation loomed closer, Mazepink considered what direction he wanted his life to take. "I went home from the shop one night with a bottle of wine and asked myself that most basic question: 'If I could do anything for the rest of my days what would I do?' I got lucky when I came up with an immediate answer: I wanted to pursue winemaking."

Chris flew out to California and Oregon to review the winemaking programs at UC Davis and the Oregon State University. "I was captivated by the natural beauty here in Oregon," he recalls, "so I ended up studying viticulture at Oregon State in Corvallis." That was 17 years ago.

Chris began his career as assistant winemaker at Lemelson Vineyards, in Carlton, Oregon. He spent four years at Shea Wine Cellars, in Newberg, where he tripled case production and fine-tuned their blends, then joined Benton-Lane Winery, in Monroe, as their director of winemaking and viticulture. With years of experience running a large estate devoted to ultra-premium Pinot Noir, Chris came to Archery Summit in 2013. "I firmly believe that the best wines in Oregon are made from the Dundee Hills and Ribbon Ridge AVAs," he says. "At Archery Summit we have all the ingredients to build upon the winery's past successes."

Throughout our interview with Chris, he was very respectful of Gary Andrus and paid tribute to what Andrus achieved at Archery Summit. "Our whole concept of Archery Summit was inspired by Pine Ridge in Napa's Stags Leap and Gary Andrus," Chris told us.

"Gary planted a lot of clones and rootstocks and experimented with row orientations and vine densities. He really extracted the wines when they were in tank and he had great success. He used lots of vigorous punch downs and even utilized a lot of oak, sometimes 100 percent new. He also favored whole-cluster fermentation. His ultimate goal was to have this estate produce the best possible new-world Pinot Noir, emulating, in many ways, DRC [Domaine de la Romanée-Conti—an estate in Burgundy, France, making what some consider the best wines in the world]. He had a lot of commercial success with the wines he made, but then, after he left, the winery went through a period where the wines backed off in ripeness, concentration, and structure because of a different winemaking approach. Since I came here, we've gone full circle, back to the original style. There are a lot of similarities between Gary's style and mine."

Pinot Noir grapes harvested by hand.

It's Not About You

"If I had to choose whether I'm going to be in the winery or working in the vineyard, I'll always pick the vineyard," says Chris. "I love being out there, I love being on the tractor, and I love walking up and down the vines." And he clearly loves the challenge of growing the finicky Pinot Noir grape. "In my mind the Pinot Noir grape is a little time capsule that mirrors its entire six months of growing on the vine," he says. "It reflects more about where it's from than any other grape. The trials and tribulations of growing are what builds character in a wine; struggle is essential in making complex Pinot Noir."

For Chris, producing Pinot Noir is unlike making any other wine. "Pinot Noir is a very cerebral varietal that should cause some contemplation, reflection, and curiosity," he insists, though he is preaching to the choir when talking to us about this subject. "When you first smell and then taste Pinot Noir, you should be continually trying to figure out that elusive note you've just experienced. Pinot Noir is not just some average quaffable beverage. A wine like Cabernet is more about the person making it. If you try to make Pinot about 'you,' you've already lost the battle."

An Interesting Evolution

The wine industry in Oregon has changed a lot since Chris first arrived, two decades ago. "I tend to avoid the Burgundy vs. Oregon references," he says. "Ten years ago we used to talk

Above: **Archery Summit's vineyards in the Dundee Hills.**
Pages 200–201: **The Looney Vineyard at sunset.**

about our wines more in relation to Burgundy or California. Now we just compare Oregon to Oregon, which has been an interesting evolution in the industry. I don't know if it will be like this 20 years from now, but I can tell you the way we have become globally recognized in one lifetime is by having a very collegial, open, and collaborative industry. If my press breaks during the harvest I can call Véronique Drouhin and she will say, 'Come on up, you can press your grapes here.' It's not like that in places like Napa."

Many winemakers have spoken to us about the collaborative spirit of winemaking in Oregon and how it has helped propel the wine to superior heights. Yet most winemakers, like Mazepink, think that Oregon winemaking still has a long way to go. "It would be naïve to think we've tapped in to everything Oregon has to offer," cautions Chris. "Only 2 percent of the state's acreage has been turned into wine grapes, so there's a lot of vineyard land still out there just waiting to be developed. If you want to plant 100 acres, you can

**Chris Mazepink (center) with authors
Nick Wise and Linda Sunshine.**

Méo Camuzet—and of course the Drouhins have been here for a long time. More of them are coming. I am sure we will soon have world-class Chardonnay, but at half the price. Twenty years from now we will look at Oregon Pinot Noir and Chardonnay the same way that today we look at Burgundy."

We asked Chris about a recent Silicon Valley poll that claimed 43 percent of the wineries in Oregon suspect they will try to sell their vineyards in the next five years. "It's because these founding families don't always have a succession plan or family interest in continuing on," he says. "What will happen when this big chunk of properties comes on the market? What we're seeing now with Jadot and Kendall Jackson is that they're realizing the relative value here, especially compared to plots in Napa."

Of course, no one can predict the future but everyone can acknowledge that Oregon winemaking has come an awfully long way and that there are major changes on the horizon. The Oregon wine business celebrated its 50th anniversary in 2016; that is 50 years since the first known vines were planted here. For a long time, no one took Oregon wines very seriously. "Today I can go to Hong Kong or the UK and Oregon Pinot Noir is known," Mazepink says with pride. "We hope we are the pacesetters."

We think it's fair to say that Oregon has raised the bar pretty high in the production of world-class wines. Future winemakers here, whether following in the footsteps of their families, starting from scratch, or developing plots for big corporations, will have a lot to emulate and a uniquely precious heritage to preserve.

do that here. In Burgundy, all the land has been taken. And Napa is far too expensive. Here, if you want to try something new and plant an experimental vineyard, you can go for it!"

Mazepink also agrees with winemakers like Rollin Soles and other local vintners who see a bright future for Chardonnay in the Willamette Valley. "There is a sea of Chardonnay out there, but only a small number of places in the world that do it great," he explains. "I believe this will be one of them, like the Côte de Beaune. There are so many French *vignerons* who are taking notice of Oregon as a world-class spot for growing Pinot and Chardonnay—Jadot, Lafon,

NICK'S TASTING NOTES

2013 Renegade Ridge Pinot Noir, Dundee Hills

Planted on the eastern slope of the estate, the Renegade Ridge vineyard has been biodynamically farmed since 2004. This wine is ripe and tangy, open and mouthwatering, with fresh, bright red-fruit flavors of loganberries, red cherries, cranberries, and redcurrants. Medium bodied, it is elegant, silky, and smooth on the palate with racy acidity and light tannins. The fruit is pure and focused yet broad without lashings of oak. It ends long with a bright citrus finish. The distinct orange-peel note that weaves its way throughout this wine makes it a succulent Pinot Noir for short-term drinking. The vineyard produced 582 cases.

2013 Archer's Edge Pinot Noir, Dundee Hills

Archer's Edge is Archery Summit's newest vineyard in the Dundee Hills. Planted in 2007, the 10-acre, south-facing, primarily volcanic plot on the eastern part of the estate can, in warm vintages, produce quite a dark rendition of the Pinot Noir grape. This wine was born from the unusual 2013 vintage and presents a more immediate, open red raspberry and red cherry fruit character with a strong sinewy vein of black fruit winding its way through the wine's core. Clean and elegant with slightly lower acidity than the Renegade Ridge, this is nonetheless a high-toned wine, exhibiting racy acidity and grainy tannins, ensuring there is more to come with extended cellar time. A slightly exotic spicy edge adds extra interest. A total of 6,451 cases were produced.

2013 Red Hills Pinot Noir, Dundee Hills

Archery Summit is entering "fine wine" territory with this very serious Pinot Noir. Dark and rich, there's a big jump in complexity with this cuvée. Starts off strong with a deep ruby-crimson color that leads on to a spicy bouquet. There's a lot going on here: aromas of red velvet-cake marzipan, mint, and wild savory forest notes mingle with the blackberry and strawberry fruits. Smooth and silky, yet concentrated with racy acidity and firm, sweet small-grained tannins, this is a long, lush, and fruity wine with time in hand; best left in the cellar for 5 to 8 years.

2015 Looney Pinot Noir, Ribbon Ridge

Another cuvée that provides a much darker glimpse of the Pinot Noir grape. The Looney Vineyard is young and the wines from the sedimentary soils of the Ribbon Ridge region are very different than the volcanic soils that are found at the Archery Summit Estate vineyards. The wines produced from Ribbon Ridge usually have a distinct dark-fruit quality compared to the bright red character of the Dundee Hills wines. The faster growing, warmer soils from this vineyard produce succulent, juicy fruited wines that are quite New World in style with a certain sense of lushness and a broadness to their ripe fruit. Medium bodied and vibrant due to its high acidity, this wine has firm, brawny tannins buried beneath the wealth of smooth mouthwatering fruit, black tea, and *sous-bois* flavors. The cuvée has good mineral length and, once again, a distinct orange-rind note; best left in the cellar for 5 to 8 years.

2015 Arcus Estate Pinot Noir, Dundee Hills

The Arcus Vineyard includes some of the oldest Pinot Noir vines in the Willamette Valley and produces opulent wines with a sweetly ripe mélange of red and black fruits but also an overriding and distinct floral character. I found that this wine had some well-needed crunchy high-toned red fruits, black tea, and citrus notes lurking in the background, providing lift and complexity. It has good structure, an excellent depth of fruit, and a distinct long floral finish. Drink in 5 years; 735 cases were produced.

2015 Whole Cluster Cuvée Pinot Noir, Dundee Hills

This wine dazzles on both the nose and palate, releasing a potpourri of wild red-berry forest fruit aromatics that mingle with more exotic aromas of bouquet garni, fresh white mountain flowers, dried flowers, porcini mushrooms, meat juices, Christmas cake, and cloves. The palate is smooth, silky, and seamless yet concentrated, with caressing medium-bodied red and black fruits, sweet medium tannins, and of course a high-toned, crisp, very long mineral-infused finish.

2005 Arcus Estate Pinot Noir, Dundee Hills

This bottle (a gift from Chris) was a real treat and opened our eyes to the amazing mid-term aging potential of Oregon wines; they positively demand cellar time to come together and gain weight and complexity. 2005 was a very warm year and this Pinot Noir reveals the vintage traits on all points. A dark black coffee-colored hue leads to a very broad, superbly aged, complex, savory palate. Dark, ripe, earthy flavors of smooth, velvety black cherries, redcurrants, black plums, exotic spices such as licorice, coffee beans, and a boat load of glycerin coat the palate. Layers of sappy, ripe black cherry fruits take the taster down a spindly tannic staircase until a blast of latent acidity brings one back to the surface and leads to a spice-laced, endlessly flavored finish. This wine is drinking superbly now.

ARCHERY SUMMIT

18599 NE Archery Summit Road
Dayton, Oregon 97114
503.864.4300
info@archerysummit.com
www.archerysummit.com

Tasting Room: open daily from 10am to 4pm
Tours and Private Tastings: by appointment; call or email to schedule

2014

PATRICIA GREEN CELLARS

ESTATE VINEYARD
ETZEL BLOCK

PINOT NOIR
RIBBON RIDGE

Chapter 13

The Patty and/or Jim Road Show

PATRICIA GREEN CELLARS

Newberg

For many years, we've discussed the idea of writing a book about women winemakers. If we were to limit that topic to just Oregon, it would be a very short book indeed. Even though it has been said that women have a more refined palate and are better at tasting wine, winemaking is traditionally a man's game. Until very recently, female winemakers were barely tolerated and often mistrusted. Because of this, it is unusual for a woman to name a winery after herself. This is why Patricia Green is so special to us: she uses her full name on her label, staking a claim to her rightful place in the wine world.

In our time in the Willamette Valley, we met two women winemakers—Luisa Ponzi and Patricia Green—and they could not have been more different. Whereas Luisa grew up on and then inherited her family winery, Patty Green taught herself how to make wine and then proceeded to carve out her place in this male-dominated world. She has become one of the most important names in Oregon winemaking, and we are quite certain that, like any woman in a largely male profession, she has

Patricia Green.

had to work twice as hard as any man to get where she is today.

You may not have heard of Patricia Green Cellars. The only place we'd ever seen the wine

Patricia Green Cellars' Medici Vineyard.

was on very high quality wine lists in restaurants. Though Patricia Green Cellars is a small winery with limited production, once you taste the Pinot Noir, you'll absolutely want to do what we do: order online for home delivery.

Place Matters A Lot

At Patricia Green Cellars, we discovered wine that is authentic, serious, and connected to the earth. This is Burgundian-style wine made in a new-world way. While Steve Doerner is creating old world-style Burgundian wines with "just a little touch of corruption," as he puts it, Patty Green is making flawless Burgundian wines—among the cleanest and best in the Willamette Valley.

Patricia Green Cellars produces what they describe in their newsletter as "... a crazy number of bottlings because of our intent on showing the nature of the site as the preeminent characteristic of our Pinots ... this is simply the history of Pinot Noir as done by Burgundy. However, there are reasons beyond this that lead us to the decisions we make and have made over the years, which is about who we are and where we came from. Place matters a lot. The origin of things plays a huge role in what they are and what they will become over time."

We, too, are big advocates of the importance

of terroir in the making of wine. Thus, we were psyched to meet with Patricia Green and talk about how she came to be producing such stellar wines.

A Fellow Dog Lover

The first thing we noticed when we arrived at the Newberg winery was a large enclosed pen with a half dozen dogs on the lower part of the property. We're dog lovers ourselves and always travel with Linda's peek-a-poo, Bernie. One of the pups was the spitting image of Nick's Parson Jack Russell, Lily. If Patricia was as much a dog person as we were, we knew we'd get on famously.

Exiting the car, we were greeted by Caroline Schoonveld, who runs the tasting room. She whisked us off to a barrel tasting she was conducting with two customers from New York. The barrel room was in a barnlike structure where they were setting up for their 2015 Futures Barrel Selection Dinner that evening. Lucky members of their wine club with reservations could participate in an extended barrel tasting and then pre-order the wines they liked at least a year before they were available in bottle.

Then Caroline escorted us to the recently renovated main house and the tasting room, which seemed to serve a double purpose as the living room to the house. Unlike the glitz and glamour of places like Ponzi or Domaine Serene,

Stella (left) and Blaze, two of the many beautiful creatures at Patricia Green Cellars.

**Patricia Green (center) with her staff
(from left to right): Caroline Schoonveld, Margaret
Barry, Matthew Russell, and Melissa Groshong.**

It was hard to keep pace with her energetic stride. For the next two hours, Patty never stopped moving. This was the only interview we ever conducted while on the run. Call it a moveable feast.

From the very start we could see she was a force of nature. We'd heard stories that she'd worked in many male-dominated trades, such as tree planting, construction, and sailboat crewing, and we wanted to know more. Despite the confidence of her stride in the vineyard, we sensed her shyness in talking about herself. And she definitely did not want us taking any photographs of her. "I am not a big fan of having my picture taken," she said, adding, "I'm serious," just in case we didn't get the message. We had always shot freely during our interviews, but we put away the cameras. However, when she wasn't looking, Julie, our photographer, snapped a few photos. (Sorry Patty, we couldn't help ourselves.)

As a young woman in her twenties, Patty worked in the forestry business, winning contracts by outbidding the most experienced middle-aged men. "I was working in the woods, making a lot of money. We'd go to Alaska and plant trees in Wrangell. We'd do reforestation and, you know, for a six-hour day, we could make $700 or $800. But by around 1986, I needed a career change," she said as her gaze wandered over the vines. "I had a friend who was working in the Umpqua Valley, down near Roseburg. She said I should come out and check the place out, so I took her up on her offer."

Patty began picking grapes for Richard Sommer at HillCrest Vineyard, Oregon's oldest

this felt like an invitation to visit Patty's home (although we have no idea whether or not she lived here—it just felt like someone did). As we climbed the steps, Patty Green came barreling outside to greet us with a firm handshake. "Come on," she said, with a wave of her hand. "I was thinking we could take a walk. I want to show you the vineyard."

We trotted along, scrambling up the hill to keep up with her.

A Long and Winding Path

Patty Green is small, compact and blond; a country girl stomping through the fields in her Wellingtons, clearly at home in the vineyards.

winery, in 1986. She's a girl who loves the outdoors, so the job appealed to her. "The following year, I decided I wanted to work inside the winery," she said. "My friend said I couldn't handle it because I was too small. I needed to remind her I'd been working in Alaska, planting trees. So, she hired me, and a year later, she fired the winemaker and put me in charge full-time."

Green took some classes at UC Davis but found she could learn more from working in the fields and listening to such mentors as David Adelsheim, Ted Casteel, and Richard Ponzi. "At HillCrest, I made Cabernet, Zinfandel, Pinot Noir, Merlot, Riesling, Semillon, and Sauvignon

Top: **Young grape clusters on the vine.**
Above: **The outdoor fermentation tanks and picking bins.**

Blanc. I made everything. In 1990 and 1991, I worked for Dave Adelsheim during harvest and that's when I really started to develop a better appreciation for Pinot Noir. And, as an amazing bonus, Dave sent me and his winemaker to Burgundy. I tasted the nineties vintages out of the barrel in Burgundy. Oh man, I wish I could go back," she sighed. "Anyway, that really changed the direction of my life."

She made wine for La Garza Cellars in southern Oregon and then caught a lucky break when she found a new job in 1993. "I was looking for more work, and I answered an ad in the *Wine Country* classifieds for a position at Torii Mor in McMinnville," she explained. "The owner hadn't started the winery yet and needed help."

Jim Anderson.

She got the job, and two years later, hired Jim Anderson to work at Torii Mor—a decision that would change the course of her career. Eventually, she and Jim left Torii Mor to form a partnership that would continue for the next 21 years (and is still going strong today). "Jim and I left Torii Mor in 2000," explained Patty, "when we bought an existing winery called Autumn Wind, where Jim had once worked." The owners, Tom and Wendy Kreutner, were eager to sell to Jim and his partners. "It was a turnkey operation," Patty added. "I mean, we took everything—the business, the cellar, the vineyard and all the equipment. The vineyards were planted with a lot of Pinot Noir, and there was also Chardonnay and some Sauvignon Blanc."

A True Partnership

Since then, Green and Anderson have worked side by side. Though they have very unique personalities, their differences make for a great partnership. "Our palates are similar, our goals are together. It has been really good for Jim and me because he will pick up on things I don't and I pick up on things he doesn't," Patty said.

The two share a simple philosophy about winemaking: interfere as little as possible and do only what needs to be done. Together they have come to realize that the hardest thing to do is the simplest: not much at all. With minimal manipulation of the wines, terroirs and vintages can express themselves. These efforts have led them to produce vineyard-designated Pinot Noirs from well-farmed, high-quality sites, thus creating uniquely individual wines.

Above: **The small farm tractor fits perfectly between the vines.**
Pages 214–215: **The vineyard in early autumn when the leaves start to turn color.**

The entire winery is dedicated fully and solely to producing Pinot Noirs that reflect where they are grown. All the vineyards are either organically or sustainably farmed to produce textures, aromatics, and flavors that are site-specific. Patty's wines are made to be approachable in the short term yet also built for longevity. "We have more of a feminine style of winemaking," explained Patty. "We are not heavy hitters in terms of extraction, unless we have a big vintage in which we have no choice, like 2003." Her method hasn't changed very much over the years though she does think it has become more fine-tuned. Green and Anderson are so focused on place, they've designed their labels to emphasize the vineyard and block where the grapes are grown, even more than the name of the winery.

Green acknowledged that wine takes on the character of its producers, a point we've made many times in our books. "Wines are a lot like the personality of the people who make

them," said Green. "If you put so much of your personal, mental, and physical energy into making wine, I think it really translates into the wines."

Clearly, Anderson and Green respect and enjoy working together. He pointed out that Patty has a keen sense of humor, adding, "She is also very intuitive—in the vineyard and in the winery. Her wines are very well balanced and great with food. But her best asset is that she has developed a great nose. I think it benefits her more than tasting." Explaining their wines, Jim told us, "Our style is in the vineyard."

In a company newsletter, Anderson, a formidable writer with a wicked sense of humor, provided perhaps the best description we've ever read of what it takes to become a great Pinot Noir winemaker. "Being peculiar is hardly a personality trait that one casually puts on a resume," he wrote, "but non-linear thinking, questioning established ideals, going about things in less than traditional ways and, in general, being somewhat odd has the capacity to serve one well in the stewardship of Pinot Noirs."

The Patty and/or Jim Road Show

"The industry has changed in the past 10 years," said Patty, as we continue trudging up the hill. "It's really grown and today there is more of a global competition for wine. It's not like 20 years ago, when we didn't do any marketing. Now Jim and I spend the first part of the year on the road."

Jim elaborated on these changes, again displaying a wry sense of humor. "The making of wine comes with the inevitable issue of selling the wine," he wrote. "We are neither running a wine museum nor have the personal fortunes to simply make wine and stash the lion's share of it in some warehouse à la the end of *Raiders of the Lost Ark*. I would say that both of these things are unfortunate (especially the personal fortune part and the lack thereof). We are not so artisanal and introverted that we don't actually get a measure of enjoyment out of the sales end of the deal ... For probably the first seven vintages we produced, we rarely traveled or really even had to travel. There was the occasional trip to Chicago, New York, Seattle and that was about it. Honestly, there was no great need for the Patty and/or Jim roadshow."

This was perhaps because their starting operation was around 5,000 cases (today they are producing more than twice that amount) and back in 2000, there were far fewer competing wines and wineries in Oregon than there are now. Yet Anderson doesn't complain about the competition; instead he explained how they've taken on the responsibility that comes with competing for sales. "Over the past seven years or so we have stepped up our traveling," he said. "We are still either stubborn enough or just flat-out stupid enough that we don't have a person in charge of this aspect of the business. Ninety percent of the out-of-state wine marketing and selling is still done by Patty and myself." Without a dedicated salesperson, the two winemakers can only do so much about distribution and the wines are currently only available in 25 states and a handful of foreign countries. But they are making a special kind of wine for a particular consumer.

"The sort of wines we dabble in are still a fraction of the much larger wine market," admitted Jim. "However, as people are becoming more interested in where, how, and by whom their food is grown and produced, it is clear they are also more interested in the same questions about their wines. We see an increasing demand for wines that are made from vineyards that are organically and sustainably farmed in ways that are respectful of the land and fruit and that taste good, age well, and ultimately have a connection to the place from where they came. This may seem obvious to many people, but it is just short of revolutionary to be happening across the breadth of this huge country."

We couldn't agree more. In our travels, we have consistently witnessed the expanding interest in farm-to-table dining and wine appreciation.

Happy Anniversary

Last year, Patricia Green Cellars celebrated its 15th anniversary and it was a time of evolution and growth. A more modern, clean, and elegant wine label was created. The tasting room was remodeled, making it possible to host

Grapes on the vine at Patricia Green Cellars' Durant Vineyard.

tastings six days a week (though reservations are required). A long-awaited new sign was added to the property. Change is good, we will all generally agree, but it is also stressful. "So while we had a productive and positive year, one always wonders whether there is a pot of gold or dried up dog poop at the end of the rainbow of change," wrote Anderson. "That can lead to long nights and hard looks at one's self and those are never easy things to face. How and when do you know if what you've done is not only successful but also, in the end, what you really wanted to do?"

The answer may lie in the wines themselves.

"The most interesting wines, in my mind, are still made by feel, instinct, experience, know-how, and with simple refined techniques," explained Jim. "Life, how you go about it and perceive what is going on, is much the same way ... We have been around for 15 years and haven't forgotten the value of staying firmly rooted in what we do while still pushing and expanding our borders."

A Special Spot

Back in the vineyard with Patty, we neared the top of her property, our final destination. It seemed like the perfect moment to ask Patty how she felt about the success she has achieved as a woman in a man's world, but she seemed uninterested in the question, clearly having been asked it many times. "I've worked in male-dominated industries my entire life, so entering this one was no different," she said with a shrug. "People always ask me what it's like being a woman in this business and, honestly, I don't really think about it. I look back now and see it was tough. But when I was immersed in it, I didn't think I was getting singled out. I was friendly and most people were friendly back."

Ambitious and hardworking, it seems as though she has kept herself focused, doing what needed to be done without worrying what other people thought. She carved out a unique and creative life that perfectly suits her skills, interest, and personality. We think it's safe to say that the winery is Patty's manifestation of living a life that has been free of self- or gender-imposed restrictions.

Finally, after what seemed like an arduous climb, we reached the apex of her property, that special spot overlooking the valley and her neighboring winery, Beaux Frères. This was the place she particularly loves and wanted to show us. "I like to come up here with a bottle of wine when I am feeling stressed out," Patty told us, and it is easy to understand why. Here was a most peaceful and inspiring place with a forest of green on the horizon. Amid all those beautiful, well-tended, and carefully nurtured grapevines, one can only imagine the sense of accomplishment and pride she must feel. There aren't many people, let alone women, who can gaze out over such lush and verdant fields and think, "This is what I've built."

Artist Lyle Railsback painted portraits of several Oregon winemakers; Patty's was used on a bottling to commemorate the winery's 15th anniversary.

15TH ANNIVERSARY
15
CUVÉE

PATRICIA GREEN CELLARS

2014 Sauvignon Blanc

There isn't much Sauvignon Blanc in the Willamette Valley but Patricia Green's is one of the best. The wine displays a water-white/light straw color with pure fresh notes of tangy grapefruit, grass, guava, and stone fruit on the palate. Doesn't lean particularly toward an herbal or tropical style but sits deftly in the middle. This wine is easy to drink, refreshing, pure, flavorsome, and lithe, with adequate acidity and a long finish.

2014 Notorious Pinot Noir, Willamette Valley

This is a personal favorite—and the most exotic—of the three special Pinot Noirs made at Patricia Cellars. As Patty says of this wine, "[Rather than] attempting to show, in painstaking detail, the individual qualities of the vineyards, our work with the Notorious bottling is about a particular style of wine that is richer, more intense, denser in texture, and more lifted aromatically than our other bottlings. It is made in 100 percent new Cadus barrels. As always this wine is a textural experience beyond any of our other wines." Supremely complex, this black-fruited wine is phenomenal on both the palate and the nose. Exotic scents of spices, oak, and earth set the scene before the velvety, powerful Pinot hits and coats the palate—smooth and silky but a with great depth of lush fruit, while the acidity keeps it lively. Long in the mouth, it has a very promising future. The last six Notorious vintages (2007–2012) have received scores of 94, 93, 94, 93, 94 and 95 from *International Wine Cellar*.

2005 Whistling Ridge Vineyard Pinot Noir, Ribbon Ridge

This wine displays a dark crimson color with a browning rim. The bouquet opens with a medium-intense mélange of red and black mineral fruits, earth, and spice but sits predominantly in the black fruit corner compared to the 2002 Reserve, which shows brighter red fruits.

2002 Reserve Pinot Noir, Willamette Valley

This is the first vintage released of this wine. It displays a medium-dark crimson color and an expressive nose that's now quite tertiary, exuding aromas of earthy red forest fruits, strawberry jam, and briary raspberry tart. Elegant and delicate in the mouth, it has a velvet character with ripe flavors of raspberry, spice, currant, earth, and cinnamon, which are supported by a tangy acidity and fine-grained light tannins.

PATRICIA GREEN CELLARS

15225 North Valley Road
Newberg, Oregon 97132
503.554.0821
tasting@patriciagreencellars.com
www.patriciagreencellars.com

Tasting Room: open Monday to Saturday for tastings at 10am, 11:30am, and 2:30pm, by appointment only

Chapter 14
The French Connection

Opposite: **The wine label wall at the Joel Palmer House, in Dayton.**
Above: **A barrel from Domaine Drouhin Oregon.**

It was only a matter of time before the French, producers of the world's highest-quality Pinot Noir, discovered Oregon's Willamette Valley. Conversely, it only made sense for American winemakers to reach out to their French counterparts to help cultivate the wines of Oregon and bring their old-world experience, knowledge, and expertise to the New World.

In Burgundy, where winemaking dates back almost 1,500 years, every inch of land legally available for growing grapes has long been occupied. In order to expand, the French have to look elsewhere, which is why they've been exploring winemaking regions from the Australian Coast to Croatia and every possible area in between. Pinot Noir can flourish only in a particular environment, and the French have come to realize that Oregon is one of those special places. The first French winemaker to invest in the Willamette Valley was Robert Drouhin, of Maison Drouhin, who arrived here even before the first Oregon wines were bottled.

DOMAINE DROUHIN OREGON

Dayton

Pages 224–225 and above: **Landscape views of the vineyards at Domaine Drouhin Oregon.**

Maison Joseph Drouhin was founded in 1880, when Burgundian winemaker Joseph Drouhin moved from Chablis to Beaune. In 1957, his grandson, Robert Drouhin, became the third generation to run the business. He "discovered" Oregon on a 1961 visit, years before the pioneering families arrived in the valley. The region came onto Drouhin's radar again during the 1979 and 1980 blind tastings in Paris and Burgundy that validated Oregon wines on an international scale. Drouhin recognized that, more so than California, Oregon's soil and climate could unlock the potential of Pinot Noir and Chardonnay in the United States.

In 1987, Drouhin was invited to participate in the first International Pinot Noir

Welcome to the tasting room at DDO.

Celebration (IPNC) in McMinnville, and on that trip, he decided to purchase land that was previously farmed for wheat and Christmas trees in the Dundee Hills. At the same time, Robert appointed his daughter Véronique Boss-Drouhin, a fourth-generation winemaker, to be the winemaker for Domaine Drouhin Oregon (DDO). Véronique brought a wealth of local experience to the position (after having obtained her wine diploma in France, she worked at Adelsheim, Eyrie Vineyard, and Bethel Heights). At the same time, her brother, Philippe Drouhin, took responsibility for viticulture at the winery. In 1988, DDO produced its first vintage, from purchased grapes, and in 1989 built their landmark four-story gravity-flow winery. The Drouhins now possess more than 180 acres of land in the Côte d'Or and more than 279 acres in the heart of the Willamette Valley.

In 2012, Véronique explained the difference between Oregon and Burgundy Pinot Noir to Katie Kelly Bell of *Forbes* magazine. "Oregon wines have a darker color with spicy nuances,

notes of currant, and very silky tannins," said Véronique. "The challenge in Oregon is to maintain elegance in the wine. The challenge in Burgundy, where the wines are always elegant, is to produce a wine with some weight. The two together would make a perfect wine."

Véronique's high-quality wines age superbly and reflect a classic Burgundian style of winemaking. Her Pinot Noirs are dark, slick, and well textured, with a good lashing of sweet oak paired to an impeccably structured frame. DDO's expertise in winemaking has also made them one of the leaders in the race to introduce world-class white wines from Oregon to the market. In 2013, DDO purchased the stunning Roserock Vineyard in the Eola-Amity Hills, and so the Drouhin story continues.

Elegant etched goblet from DDO.

EVENING LAND VINEYARDS

Dundee

Evening Land tasting room, in Dundee.

While Robert Drouhin invested in Oregon land to expand DDO, the Hollywood producer Mark Tarlov brought two brilliant and renowned French winemakers to Oregon to shape both of his winemaking ventures. Tarlov first came to the Willamette Valley in the mid-1990s, when he created the phenomenal Evening Land.

What motivated Tarlov to take up the risky business of winemaking? "Well, drinking," he told us, with a laugh. "And my per diem. In 1993, I made a movie in San Francisco called *Copycat* and Larry Stone had just opened his restaurant, Rubicon. Larry is a great master sommelier and a raconteur, and he sort of seduced me into the joys of French wines, not all Burgundy but mostly Burgundy, a little bit in the Rhône Valley. I became very interested and started drinking. He's the first one who showed me a Jayer wine. I thought, 'Ooh. This

is yummy!' And because we were on per diem, we could afford them."

In 2005, Tarlov hired Dominique Lafon, from the famed Domaine des Comtes Lafon in Burgundy, as his consulting winemaker. Tarlov had just purchased the extraordinary Seven Springs Vineyard in the Eola-Amity Hills. Historically, Seven Springs has produced some of the finest grapes grown in the United States and was selected as one of the "Top 10 Vineyards in America" by *Food and Wine* magazine. Lafon took advantage of the distinctive terroir of Seven Springs to produce some very interesting Pinot Noir for Evening Land. In comparing his French and Oregonian wines, Dominique Lafon said, "I've tasted the Pinot

Evening Land wines.

The historic Seven Springs Vineyard, in the Eola-Amity Hills, is considered one of the best in America.

Noir from Oregon, and it is not the same as the wines in Burgundy, but Oregon is closer in style to what we do. For me it's a matter of elegance, purity, and silkiness, not alcohol and ripe fruit. With Seven Springs, we work with the land and soil in the traditional way, looking to create the good balance in the glass."

Tarlov left Evening Land in January 2012, selling his shares to his partner, Steve Webster, while Dominique stayed on for several more years. Today Evening Land's wine stewards are Rajat Parr and Sashi Moorman. Parr, a two-time James Beard Award winner and author of *Secrets of the Sommeliers*, is internationally regarded as one of the world's foremost wine experts. As vineyards and winemaking became ever more an obsession, Parr transitioned from sommelier to producer. In 2013, he released wines from his and Moorman's estate vineyard, Domaine de la Côte, located in the Sta. Rita Hills. After Rajat and Sashi came to Evening

Land, the overall flavor profile of the wines changed toward a more direct, clean, and transparent style. Since they both hail from a food and wine background, their wines are balanced with moderate levels of alcohol, seemingly tailor-made to complement food.

As Rajat told us, "We kept Seven Springs Vineyard, which is very special to us. And now we have two very different vineyards, different soils, different climates, and it's absolutely a dream come true to see two completely different places grow Pinot Noir. Seven Springs, of course, has been historically one of the great vineyards in Oregon, while Domaine de la Côte is still young and will hopefully find its place in the world one day."

Evening Land's wines reflect a wonderful sense of purity and elegance with a precise sense of terroir. The wines are typically Burgundian in their creation but, conversely, very Oregonian with a touch more ripeness at their center.

CHAPTER 24

Dundee

Producer Mark Tarlov commissioned artist Cathie Bleck to paint a wall mural, which is titled *Fire and Flood* and hangs in the tasting room of Chapter 24.

After leaving Evening Land, Mark Tarlov created his second winery, the innovative Chapter 24. The two ventures share some common goals: both aim for Burgundian perfection and were created in conjunction with a legendary French producer. For Chapter 24, Tarlov joined forces with Viscount Louis-Michel Ligier-Belair, whose vineyard, Domaine des Comtes Ligier-Belair, in Vosne-Romanée, dates to 1815, when Napoleon granted the land to his family.

Tarlov's choice of the unique name, Chapter 24, is from Homer's epic tale, *The Odyssey*, referencing the concluding chapter when Odysseus finally returns home to the Greek island of Ithaca. Often referred to as "Reunion and Resolution," the final chapter of *The Odyssey* resolves the conflict between Odysseus and the gods so that his narrative with his wife, son, father, Poseidon, Athena, and Zeus can be reset and begin again. Chapter 24 is perhaps the most literary winery ever established and their website showcases the words of such luminaries as Lewis Carroll, Richard Feynman, Robert Louis Stevenson, Albert Einstein, and Eduardo Galeano, who wisely said, "We are all mortal until the first kiss and the second glass of wine."

In the literature available at the winery, Tarlov details his own thoughts on winemaking in a list he calls Pinot Principia, which includes such mottos as, "Think inside the box. Encourage diversity everywhere. Create a circular narrative. Embrace the paradoxes, asymmetries, and imbalances that are the natural world. Find harmonies and patterns." This is not just excellent advice for winemakers; these words also resonate in every aspect of our lives.

Where other winemakers are concentrating on site-specific wines, Chapter 24 is mixing it up, quite literally. Ligier-Belair and Tarlov now produce organic wine from across 48 sites in the five wine regions of the Willamette Valley, creating three distinctive Pinot Noir cuvées—respectively named The Fire, The Flood, and Last Chapter. Eighty parcels from 30 vineyards are designated as either "Fire" (volcanic soils) or "Flood" (marine sediment soils), while the best lots from either soil type are selected for "Last Chapter," their top bottling. Each of the three high-quality wines is fascinating in its own right. The Fire and The Flood highlight the differences in grapes grown in the older, rockier, volcanic soils as compared with those from vineyards planted in younger, richer soils. The two soils of the Willamette Valley produce wines of contrasting flavors, textures and perfumes. The volcanic Jory soils are generally found to be more masculine and mineral-driven, while grapes grown on Marine soils display a more delicate, expressive, and almost feminine quality.

Liger-Belair favors what he calls "infusion winemaking," where the whole-berry grape is fermented with a gentle infusion technique, as opposed to press extraction. The result is that the grapes can be harvested riper and produce less alcohol. (Tarlov has recently spent a year compiling scientific evidence about the system in published papers on yeast and fermentation behavior.)

Mark Tarlov believes that diversity produces complexity, and harmonious complexity produces pleasure. The whole must be greater than the sum of the parts. It's hard to argue the point when he and Liger-Belair are making such complex and delicious wines.

Chapter 24's signature Pinot Noir, "Last Chapter."

MAISON LOUIS JADOT

Yamhill – Carlton

The French invasion here continued in August 2013, when Maison Louis Jadot purchased the Résonance Vineyard, a beautiful piece of prime land in the Yamill-Carlton region. These 32 hectares sit on a sickle-curved hillside that was previously sourced by the Lemelson, Sineann, and Big Table Farm wine estates. At the time of the purchase, the president of Jadot, Pierre-Henry Gagey, told *Wine Spectator*, "We were impressed by the quality of the wines we tasted from the Résonance Vineyard."

Gagey also explained that Jadot originally had no plans to enter the Willamette Valley, but then decided to take a big leap of faith, based on their admiration for the Drouhins, especially daughter Véronique and the wines she was producing here. "Six months ago. I did not know we would be doing this," claimed Gagey. "It was not planned. We liked Oregon, we liked the property, and we liked Kevin Chambers (the original owner). It's as simple as that. All the pieces in the puzzle fit together."

Jacques Lardière, who had retired as Jadot's technical director in 2012, was assigned to oversee the Oregon operation. Lardière told *Wine Spectator* he was surprised and challenged to discover that the vines in Résonance Vineyard were on their original rootstocks. Previously, he had worked only on grafted vines.

Jadot's Pinot Noir cuvée is named Résonance after the vineyard. It is a very high quality and quite age-worthy wine, possessing a proud Oregonian character with a touch of Burgundy.

For now, Jadot has no winery in the region. Further ventures here are possible in the future. "We're going to take our time and do things step by step, little by little," said Gagey. "We need to understand the terroir and culture of Oregon first."

Pinot Noir grapes ready for harvesting.

NICOLAS·JAY

Yamhill

The most recent French winemaker to stake a claim in Oregon soil is Jean-Nicolas Méo of Domaine Méo-Camuzet, in the village of Vosne-Romanée, one of Burgundy's top producers. Méo learned his craft from the legendary Henri Jayer and spent 30 years working in Burgundy's greatest vineyards. Méo has been interested in Oregon since he attended the IPNC in 1991. "I loved the valley's Burgundy-like charm and mentality, with its dedicated farmers and small, family-run wineries committed to making wines of great character," he says.

Jean-Nicolas joined forces with music executive Jay Boberg to create a wine named for their friendship. Boberg cofounded the seminal Indie record label, I.R.S. Records, and became the president of MCA/Universal Records, launching or fostering the careers of such artists as R.E.M., the Go-Go's, Blink-182, Mary J. Blige, Sublime, the Roots, and B. B. King. He is currently chairman of Isolation Networks, parent of digital music provider INgrooves and digital book publisher INscribe.

In the early 1990s, Boberg owned a vineyard in Napa Valley. "There are so many parallels between music and wine," explains Jay. "Both are driven by personal recommendations—one friend telling another—and they both enhance and enrich our lives by creating emotional connections. There are certain wines, like certain albums, that move and stay with

Jay Boberg and Jean-Nicolas Méo.

you forever." Like Jean-Nicolas, Jay has been a fan of Oregon wines for decades. "People used to talk about their potential, but now you can taste what that potential has become—earth and elegance," he says.

Boberg and Méo have been friends since 1988. "We share similar philosophies about life, business, wine, and friendship," says Jay. "Nicolas-Jay is about making the very best Pinot Noir we can possibly make. It is also about building something together that one day we hope our kids will be a part of. When you look at the great *domaines* of the world, these two ideas go hand in hand."

Initially, Boberg and Méo thought buying a vineyard wouldn't be affordable. "When we started looking, we realized that land wasn't

that expensive," says Méo. "Some colleagues showed us a wine from the Bishop Creek Vineyard, which was the best we had tasted. The vineyard was for sale and the relatively modest 15 acres was manageable for us. It had no irrigation, had tight spacing for Oregon, a good aspect, and was old [at 28 years] by Oregon standards, but most importantly, we liked the wines produced there."

The purchase price of the entire vineyard was less than the cost of a single hectare (about 2.5 acres) in the best Burgundian vineyards. The fruit they source to produce other vintages comes from almost every AVA in the Willamette Valley, including sites in the high elevation Eola-Amity Hills, the cool coastal range in McMinnville, and the red soils of the Dundee Hills. Nicolas-Jay released their first 2014 vintage in 2016, and their future goal is to release a 2017 Chardonnay.

The incredible soil of the Willamette Valley.

Change is the Law of Life

Nicolas-Jay is the fifth vineyard in the Willamette Valley to unite well-known Burgundian winemakers with Oregon soil. Méo is in excellent company, joining a very elite group that includes Véronique Drouhin, at Domaine Drouhin Oregon; Dominique Lafon, formerly at Evening Land Vineyards; Jacques Lardière, at Louis Jadot's Résonance Vineyard; and Louis-Michel Liger-Belair, at Chapter 24.

There is no denying the enormous influence the French have had and continue to exert in the Willamette Valley. They are bringing old-world charm and elegance to the New World, and local winemakers have reaped enormous benefits from the cross-pollination of ideas, styles, and techniques. The "French Invasion" that started with the Drouhin family will stretch well into the future.

And the Willamette Valley will continue to evolve as more and more established winemakers and curious novices come for a visit and decide to stay. As John F. Kennedy once said, "Change is the law of life. And those who look only to the past or present are certain to miss the future." No one here seems to be stuck in the past or even wedded to the present. Innovation is welcomed and celebrated. Everyone seems to be looking for ways to improve and enhance what they've already created. Surely, no one here is going to miss out on the future.

Opposite: **Boberg and Méo at their Bishop Creek Vineyard.**

DOMAINE DROUHIN OREGON

2012 Édition Limitée Chardonnay, Dundee Hills

Tasted at a special event at the Domaine, this Chardonnay was exemplary. Powerful, concentrated, and broad shouldered while retaining that vibrant Oregon acidity and a beautiful fine balance, this wine is neither over oaked nor syrupy, but rather expressive and elegant. Medium bodied, with a direct and pure character that pushes its sinewy vibrant flavors to the fore—while a hint of oak lurks in the background and adds a very light, comfortable layer of sweet oak for a sense of seamlessness—this wine is a serious and complex reflection of what can be achieved with the correct clone in Oregon. The melding of white fruits to minerals is precise and flavorsome; the acidity is high yet tangy; and the finish is long and lingering. Drink within 5 to 7 years. Only 149 cases were produced. Awarded 94 points by *Wine Spectator*.

2012 Pinot Noir Laurène, Dundee Hills

This powerful, broad-shouldered wine manages to retain an amazing focus and a deft balance. Fresh and lively on the nose, a mélange of red and black forest fruits, spice, light oak, and floral aromas waft from the glass. The dark, rich, concentrated, and layered palate has an amazing depth of fruit, and an incredible stretchy mid-palate leads to a huge juicy wave of fruit at the back end. Long in the mouth, it has good capacity to age for at least 10 years. A total of 2,500 cases were made.

2015 Pinot Noir Cuvée Louise, Dundee Hills

This is a rare wine made from a blend of Véronique's favorite barrels. A small production cuvée that's rarely reviewed, it's a dark, gamey style of

Pinot. Ripe black fruits are revealed at the fore, with deep throaty forest-floor aromas of black cherries, cassis, black plums, and blackberries initially taking center stage. Light aromas of creamy oak, spice, cola, flowers, orange rind, and mineral notes add interest to the bouquet. The palate is seriously complex, multidimensional, and multilayered. Plush and silky in the mouth, this wine is smooth and medium bodied but seriously concentrated. It's also wonderfully round with a soft texture that coats the palate. Tight, sweet, bold tannins lurk beneath the wine's lush fruit, and lively buoyant acidity holds the fruit in check and brings the wine to a lingering cherry liqueur finish. Drink in 8 to 15 years; only 250 cases were produced.

2009 Pinot Noir Laurène, Dundee Hills

Drouhin's flagship wine has been called "One of the Great Wines of America." This bottle was kindly given to us by Véronique to enjoy with our dinner that night and proved to be superb, nicely aged, and in great condition. It was a treat to see how the primarily dark-fruited style of Drouhin wines in Oregon were enhanced with time. On opening, the bouquet had picked up some tertiary notes but was still fresh and vibrant with great secondary savory characteristics of licorice, damp earth, and chocolate, plus a light feral note. There were 2,750 cases produced. Drink now.

EVENING LAND VINEYARDS

2007 Seven Springs Vineyard Summum Chardonnay, Eola-Amity Hills

Without a doubt, this is the best Chardonnay we tasted on our trip. A deep golden, almost greenish color leads to a still bright, clean sumptuous bouquet of fresh-cut citrus, pear, floral, truffles, yeast, and pineapples, with mineral and creamy aromas. The rich palate is fresh and quite filled out, with no signs of oxidation. High acidity provides focus and lift for the sleek, silky grapefruit, citrus, and mineral flavors that float to a light but long yeast-tinged finish. This wine is drinking beautifully with excellent texture. It received 94 points from *Wine Spectator*; 115 cases were made.

2012 Seven Springs Vineyard La Source Chardonnay, Eola-Amity Hills

Made in a less concentrated and more mineral-driven "European" style than the richer, more expansive, and deeper fruited Summum. A wonderful Chardonnay in its own right with bright, high-toned flavors of fresh citrus, pears, pineapple, green apples, and the lightest lick of oak. This medium-bodied but impressively endowed wine has excellent concentration, superb inner richness, depth of fruit, and a satiny texture. Drink within five years; 350 cases were made. This rare wine was awarded 96 points by *Wine Spectator*.

2012 Seven Springs Vineyard La Source Pinot Noir, Eola-Amity Hills

A knockout wine, if you can still find it. Delicately framed yet also retaining a beautiful depth of fruit that floats across the palate with a wonderful sense of weightlessness. Poised and focused, this wine tantalizes the senses with a cornucopia of silky, velvety but never ponderous fruit, releasing a tantalizing array of red and black sweet currant fruits. It is medium bodied yet impressively concentrated. An additional 5 to 8 years in the cellar will add complexity due to the sweet, tight-grained imbedded tannins. It was awarded 98 points by *Wine Spectator*; 1,176 cases were produced.

2015 Seven Springs Vineyard La Source Pinot Noir, Eola-Amity Hills

This was made from a strange vintage where the conditions were hot, yet it rained just before harvest. Surprisingly, those who waited managed to produce wine that not only reflected the heat of the vintage but also retained the freshness provided by the late rain. The wine opens up rich and ripe, with concentrated aromas and flavors of juicy red cherries, raspberries, and spice as well as floral scents. At the wine's heart there is a very succulent, almost jammy streak that is accented or augmented by the brightness infused by a fresh introduction of cool-climate fruits, minerality, and some uplifting zesty acidity. With time the tannins will become more integrated and the wine more complex and complete. It was awarded 93 points by *Wine Spectator*; 850 cases were produced.

2013 Seven Springs Vineyard Summum Chardonnay, Eola–Amity Hills

A top-tier Chardonnay from Seven Springs, this elixir immediately displays an exotic green-tinged color, followed by an explosion of scents: cool-climate citrus fruits, cream, pineapples, minerals, orange blossoms, truffles, and pear. It's not an overtly ripe wine but it is tremendously expressive and flavorsome. Already complex at this stage, it reveals lively flavors of citrus, pears, and green apples framed in light oak with an intriguing hint of white truffles. The well-judged acidity provides a cradle for the wine's mineral-infused fruit, which carries its juicy bounty toward a very long orange-tinged finish. This wine will improve over the next 10 years in the cellar. It received 95 points from *Wine Spectator*; 300 cases were made.

2014 Seven Springs Vineyard Summum Chardonnay, Eola–Amity Hills

This Chardonnay is obviously still in its primary stages but shows enormous potential for future development. Produced from a very warm vintage by Oregonian standards, this is quite a showy, opulent wine. It displays a light gold color with shiny, youthful reflective hints. Springy and vibrant, it exhibits exuberant scents of tangy fresh-cut lemons, hay, and sweet spicy oak overtones on the nose. Lurking in the background lie lazy broad notes of cashew, white truffles, spice, and pineapples. The palate has yet to broaden out, but give it about a year. This wine is a delight waiting to unfurl and will develop for 10 or more years, so patience is required.

CHAPTER 24

2012 The Fire Pinot Noir, Willamette Valley

The grapes for The Fire are grown on the volcanic Jory, Nekia, and Witzel soils, endowing this cuvée with a powerful mineral expression. Bright aromas of red cherry, raspberry, and red currants mingle with more tertiary notes of spice, minerals, and light vanilla oak. Fruitier and noticeably livelier than The Flood Pinot Noir, it has better definition and a more powerful, sweeter tannic frame. It is precise and taut in the mouth with an excellent concentration of loamy, high-toned, fresh red fruit that leads to a silky-smooth mineral-textured finish. Drink in 6 to 10 years. It was awarded 91 points by *Wine Spectator*; just under 1,000 cases were made.

2012 The Flood Pinot Noir, Willamette Valley

The Flood derives its name from the Willamette Valley's ocean-influenced, sedimentary soils where the grapes are grown. The wine shows slightly less concentration and has a more pronounced black-fruit character than The Fire cuvée. A perfumed nose soars with crisp red forest fruits, underpinned by a darker, earthier core of damp soil, herbs, exotic spices, minerals, cola, and floral notes plus a light hint of vanilla melded to ripe blackberries and black cherries. It is medium bodied but with a sappy concentrated mid-palate that delivers crisp black and red forest fruits wrapped in tight tannins. The wine ends long and mineral-tinged with a smoke-flecked, infused finish. Drink in 5 to 8 years. It was awarded 92 points by *Wine Spectator*; 1,358 cases were produced.

2015 The Last Chapter Pinot Noir, Willamette Valley

This cuvée utilizes grapes harvested from the highly prized Crawford-Beck, Shea, Hyland, and Eagle Crest Vineyards and releases a refined/reticent bouquet of aromas. Ripe, lush mineral-infused scents of red cherries and raspberries blend together with earthier, darker fruits. Later, the nose emanates with complex notes of pipe tobacco, spice-box, white flowers, stones, and light- to medium-strength vanilla oak. A well-structured, precise, complex, and very concentrated palate follows through and displays a lovely silky texture; excellent depth of fruit; and a smooth vanilla-tinged finish. This high-quality wine will be at its best from 2019 through 2028. The wine was awarded 94 points by *Wine Spectator*. The 2012 and 2013 Last Chapter were the only Pinot Noirs from the United States to be included in *Wine & Spirits* magazine as one of the Top 100 Wines of 2015; the 2012 was awarded 96 points and the 2013 was awarded 94 points.

MAISON LOUIS JADOT

2014 Résonance Vineyard Pinot Noir, Yamhill-Carlton

A striking, youthful, bloody crimson color leads to a beautifully scented, exotic, and complex bouquet that exudes a swirling mélange of tantalizing aromas. Fresh and floral, with light vanilla notes that release juicy scents of ripe red currants, raspberries, and black cherries. With exposure to the air, more complex aromas of licorice, eucalyptus, and *sous-bois* begin to appear. Medium bodied, yet mouth-filling and rich, this wine exhibits a lovely soft, plush, velvety texture and an excellent depth of ripe red and black fruits supported by small, strong sweet tannins and high, uplifting acidity. Super long in the mouth, this wine lingers with a tingling white and oriental spice element. Crafted for excellent midterm cellaring potential, it will drink best in perhaps 5 to 8 years; awarded 93 points in *Wine Spectator*.

NICOLAS-JAY

2014 Nicolas-Jay Bishop Creek Pinot Noir, Yamhill-Carlton

This wine has a very dark ruby-hued color—maybe the darkest of all the Pinots that we tasted in Oregon. Displaying a startling opaque core and broad, watery crimson rim that is closer to a Cabernet than a Pinot Noir, it is also one of the most "internationally styled." The bouquet bursts with new-world aromas of chocolate-covered super-ripe wild black cherries, overripe plums, and bright raspberries. Mingling with the more exotic aromas of light vanilla pod, damp earth, herbs, and local Marionberry (like a huge juicy blackberry), it's reasonably complex. For a Pinot Noir, it's positively full-bodied in the mouth, showcasing a very plush chocolate/gourmand style and a velvety slick, smooth texture. Drink now through 2024; awarded 93 points in *Wine Spectator*.

DOMAINE DROUHIN OREGON

6750 NE Breyman Orchards Road
Dayton, Oregon 97114
503.864.2700
info@domainedrouhin.com
www.domainedrouhin.com

Tasting Room: open daily from 11am to 4pm

EVENING LAND VINEYARDS

1326 N Hwy 99W, Suite 100
Dundee, Oregon 97115
503.538.4110
oregonhospitality@elvwines.com
www.eveninglandvineyards.com

Tasting Room: open daily from 10am to 5pm except major holidays; reservations are encouraged for parties of 6 or more.

CHAPTER 24

531 OR-99W
Dundee, Oregon 97115
503.487.6341
orders@chapter24vineyards.com
www.chapter24vineyards.com

Tasting Room: open Friday to Sunday from 11am to 5pm, and Monday to Thursday by appointment

NICOLAS-JAY

Bishop Creek Vineyard
23232 NW Russell Creek Road
Yamhill, Oregon 97148
info@nicolas-jay.com
www.nicolas-jay.com

Tasting Room: tastings are available by appointment only; please email info@nicolas-jay.com to schedule

Afterword

Visiting   the   Willamette   Valley

Opposite: **Pinot Noir grapes at Elk Cove Vineyards, in Gaston.**
Above: **A million shades of green at Domaine Drouhin Oregon.**

Falling in love with the Willamette Valley was easy, and in addition to the wine and people, had something to do with the color green. We live in Southern California, where a severe six-year drought has burnt our foliage and killed our lawns; we've gotten used to living with the color of dirt. Arriving in Oregon was like that moment in *The Wizard of Oz* when Dorothy opens her black-and-white door and steps into the world of Technicolor.

The Willamette Valley boasts so many vivid shades of green that it almost hurt our eyes to look out over the fields of grapevines and wild vegetation. Yes, it rains a lot, but that's why this place looks like the Garden of Eden. And why so many of our winemakers used the word "paradise" to describe their first impression of the area where they chose to live.

We also loved the rustic quality of the valley, which we believe is how Napa and Sonoma must've looked and felt 30 years ago, before every store became "artisanal," expensive foreign cars caused colossal traffic jams, and a weekend getaway required a bank loan. That's why we want to recommend a visit to the Willamette Valley *now*, while it is still relatively affordable and underdeveloped. We think this region offers something for everyone, from the sophisticated wine lover to the outdoorsy enthusiast of wide-open spaces. Though our time was limited (especially in Portland), we did have some mind-bogglingly great experiences and offer these suggestions for your trip.

Fly into the Portland airport and spend a day or two in this amazing city. "Portland is where young people go to retire," says Fred Armisen in his hilarious hit show, *Portlandia*. Indeed the city has a youthful, vibrant feel and offers first-rate food and entertainment. We stayed at the Nines, a luxury hotel with reasonable prices (when booked through Expedia). Well-located (near the discount Nike outlet store) and comfortable, the hotel features a terrific restaurant, the Urban Farmer, and the Departure Lounge, a rooftop bar with aerial views of the city. There are a dozen fantastic restaurants within walking distance of the Nines. The Imperial, located in the Hotel Lucia, was one of our absolute favorites.

Nick Wise writing tasting notes.

The Willamette Valley is about an hour drive from Portland and offers many places to stay. We booked our accommodations through Airbnb and VRBO and found wonderful houses for short-term rental. We stayed in Gaston on our first trip, which was lovely but very rural, and proved to be a bit too far from the places we wanted to visit. On our second trip, we stayed in McMinnville and were thrilled with the location. McMinnville is central to all the wineries and restaurants in the area. Plus, if you pick the right weekend, you, too, may see the thousands of people dressed in aluminum foil who flock to the town in celebration of the extraterrestrials among us.

If you are feeling adventurous and looking to stay someplace unique, check out the Vintages Trailer Resort in Dayton, which is unlike anything we'd previously seen. Situated on a 14-acre park, the Vintages rents out a collection of rare Airstreams and classic trailers with luxury amenities like terry-cloth robes, high-end mattresses, and quality linens. Pets and kids are welcome and the whole place looks funky and fun. By the by, the Vintages is about three miles down the road from the Evergreen Aviation & Space Museum, which features the Howard Hughes H-4 Hercules "Spruce Goose" and is Trip Advisor's number-one tourist attraction in McMinnville.

Linda Sunshine at Evening Land Vineyards.

As for food, you will not go hungry in this part of the world. Many of the restaurants feature farm-to-table dining with extraordinarily fresh and sophisticated cuisines. Our three favorites are the Joel Palmer House, in Dayton, the Dundee Bistro, in Dundee, and Recipe, in Newberg. We ate at these places many times and never had anything less than a fabulous meal. We also really loved the Jory restaurant at the Allison Inn and Spa, in Newberg, though the fancy prices nearly blew our budget for the week. If you are visiting Cristom and find yourself near Salem, have a meal at Amadeus and say hello to General Manager Alena Stewart for us.

And then of course there is the wine. We hope this book provides a good head start for discovering the beautiful wines this valley has to offer. Check out any of the wineries mentioned here and experiment with the hundreds of others we didn't have room to include.

Finally, we like to quote Lily Bollinger, of the J. Bollinger champagne company, when she was asked about the proper time to drink champagne. "I drink it when I'm happy and when I'm sad," said Lily. "Sometimes I drink it when I'm alone. When I have company I consider it obligatory. I trifle with it if I'm not hungry and drink it when I am. Otherwise, I never touch it—unless I'm thirsty." We could not have said it better, though we'd add we feel the same way about Oregon Pinot Noir.

Now that we've discovered the joys of wines from the Willamette Valley, we want to share it with the world. We hope you'll visit this region, raise a glass, and fall in love like we did.

Nick Wise & Linda Sunshine

Recommendations from Nick and Linda

The Nines
525 SW Morrison
Portland, Oregon 97204
877.229.9995
888.627.7208 (reservations)
www.thenines.com

Imperial Restaurant
410 SW Broadway
Portland, Oregon 97205
503.228.7222
www.imperialpdx.com

The Vintages Trailer Resort
16205 SE Kreder Road
Dayton, Oregon 97114
971.267.2130
reservations@the-vintages.com
www.the-vintages.com

The Evergreen Aviation & Space Museum
500 NE Capt. Michael King Way
McMinnville, Oregon 97128
503.434.4180
www.evergreenmuseum.org

The Joel Palmer House
600 Ferry Street
Dayton, Oregon 97114
503.864.2995
info@joelpalmerhouse.com
www.joelpalmerhouse.com

The Dundee Bistro
100-A SW 7th Street
Dundee, Oregon 97115
503.554.1650
info@dundeebistro.com
www.dundeebistro.com

Recipe
115 N Washington Street
Newberg, Oregon 97132
503.487.6853
reservations@recipeaneighborhoodkitchen.com
www.recipenewbergor.com

Jory Restaurant at the Allison Inn
2525 Allison Lane
Newberg, Oregon 97132
503.554.2526
www.theallison.com/jory-restaurant

Amadeus
135 Liberty Street
Salem, Oregon 97301
503.362.8830
www.amadeussalem.com

Opposite: **Wine tasting at Archery Summit.**
Pages 250–251: **Yellow vines at Ponzi's Aurora Vineyard.**

Appendix

The real dilemma in writing this book was lack of time to connect with all the winemakers we wanted to interview, especially at the four vineyards mentioned in this chapter. Although we were unable to include full chapters on these wine labels, we wanted to at least provide brief descriptions, tasting notes, and locations, along with our recommendation that any wine tour of the Willamette Valley should include visits to these wonderful places.

Oregon Pinot Noir grapes.

ANTICA TERRA
D u n d e e

Winemaker Maggie Harrison had the great fortune to land the holy grail of apprentice-ships under the tutelage of Elaine and Manfred Krankl at the iconic Sine Qua Non winery in Oak View, California. Maggie thought she was permanently settled in California until a phone call from friends Scott Adelson, John Mavredakis, and Michael Kramer convinced her to visit the vineyard they'd just purchased in Dundee. Twenty-six seconds after arriving among the oaks, fossils, and stunted vines at Antica Terra, she was on the phone, explaining to her husband that they would be moving to Oregon.

The geology of Antica Terra's 11-acre vineyard on a rocky hillside in the Eola-Amity Hills is extremely unusual. Here, the remains of a prehistoric seabed rise to the surface, leaving the vines to struggle, without topsoil, in a fractured mixture of sandstone sown with fossilized oyster shells. The resulting wines have won numerous awards, and in 2012 Harrison was named Winemaker of the Year by *Food and Wine* magazine.

2015 Botanica Pinot Noir

A medium translucent ruby color belies a massively expressive savory nose loaded with powerful aromas of barnyard, manure, and hung meat. With time in the glass, these scents reveal a spectrum of bright red forest fruits overlaid with an interesting feral note. This wine is complex, with a lovely feel of weightlessness. It will age well; drink in 5 to 8 years. Earned 93 points from *Wine Spectator*; 519 cases were produced.

ANTICA TERRA
979 SW Alder Street
Dundee, Oregon 97115
503.244.1748
info@anticaterra.com
www.anticaterra.com

BERGSTRÖM WINES
Newberg

Of Swedish origin, John Bergström, "The Pinot Noir Doctor," was a surgeon who retired to Portland with his wife, Karen, and five children. He had always dreamed of becoming a full-time *vigneron*, and in the 1970s, the Dundee Hills was the perfect place to start.

Today, Bergström Wines comprises five estate vineyards totaling 84 acres that span the best appellations in the Willamette Valley. With the help of his fourth son, Josh, who studied viticulture and oenology in Burgundy, John Bergström's vinous empire is one of the premiere properties in Oregon.

Josh is now the general manager, winemaker, and vineyard manager; his wife, Caroline, oversees the sales team. Their biodynamic property does not use any chemicals on the grapes. "It is all about microbiology," says Josh. "Wine is only a step away from vinegar anytime."

Wine tasting at Bergström.

The Bergström barn, as seen from their tasting room.

Tasting Notes: Bergström Wines

2015 Sigrid Chardonnay

Two bottles of this wine were opened, each tasting slightly different. On the nose, clean, fresh-cut flavors of mineral-infused lemon and lime meld to more complex aromas of flint, spices, cashew, honeycomb, and a light dusting of toasty vanilla oak. Drink now through 2020. Awarded 93 points by *Wine Spectator*; 1,100 cases were produced.

2012 Shea Vineyard Pinot Noir

Only 20 percent new oak gives this Pinot a fresh, bright, fruity vibe. The taut acidity and small powerful tannins contained within seem to capture the vibrancy of the fruit. Drink in 5 to 7 years. Awarded 93 points by *Wine Spectator*; 1,235 cases were made.

2013 Le Pré Du Col Vineyard Pinot Noir

Originating from Ribbon Ridge, this wine offers up the area's typical herby black-fruit style and floral notes lifted by high acidity. It's extremely well balanced, powerful, and will age superbly. Drink in 5 to10 years. It was awarded 95 points by *Wine Spectator*; 1,500 cases were produced.

2012 Bergström Vineyard Pinot Noir

Always a treat, Bergström's flagship bottling showcases a perfectly balanced mélange of red and black forest fruits pinned by measured high acidity, small powerful tannins, and a strong mineral presence. Layer upon layer of lush fruits coats the palate and leads to an awesome finish. This wine needs 5 to 8 years in the cellar. It received 95 points from *Wine Spectator*; 1,203 cases were produced.

2013 Homage Pinot Noir

A super cuvée made from the finest barrels in the cellar. A complex wine with aromas of raspberries, red cherries, cherry liqueur, black cherries, black plum, cracked pepper, vanilla, damp earth, and a lick of sweet oak. This Pinot has serious concentration and depth of fruit, a great sense of purity, and excellent aging potential. Cellar for at least 5 to 8 years, but will last up to 20 years.

2002 Arcus Vineyard Pinot Noir

This bottle was generously donated so that we could see how Bergström's wines aged. Showing rich and dense for a Pinot, this wine has really put on weight while retaining its elegance. Superb, complete, seamless, and tasty, with an immensely long, dry finish. Drink now. Awarded 94 points by *Wine Spectator*; 190 cases were made.

BERGSTRÖM WINES

18215 NE Calkins Lane
Newberg, Oregon 97132
503.554.0468
contactus@bergstromwines.com
www.bergstromwines.com

ELK COVE VINEYARDS
Gaston

The Campbell family moved here in 1974 and are considered among the first pioneers of the Willamette Valley. Pat and Joe Campbell met as teenagers and eventually settled in Gaston.

Pat's father, Lew, upon seeing his daughter's new property, commented, "With this soil and no water, I don't think you can grow anything here, except maybe wine grapes."

Soon after they moved into a trailer on the property, a herd of 40 Roosevelt elk bedded down in the clearing and wouldn't let the family out. Their presence, along with the protective bowl shape of the property, inspired the Campbells to name their estate Elk Cove.

The family dream was to produce artisanal cool-climate wines that rivaled the best in the world. This became a reality in 1979, when their 1978 Riesling won gold at three separate competitions in Oregon.

In 1999, Pat and Joe's son, Adam, took over as winemaker, and in 2005, the couple retired. Adam now oversees six vineyard sites with 350 planted acres, more than ten times the acreage of all Oregon vineyards in 1974.

Above: **The Campbells, circa mid-1970s.**
Pages 256–257: **Mount Richmond Vineyard, in Yamhill.**

Adam Campbell, a 2nd-generation winemaker.

Tasting Notes: Elk Cove Vineyards

2014 Goodrich Pinot Noir

A lovely, sensual wine, with a succulent, high-toned palate and pinpoint balance. The tannins are sweet and ripe, adding good support and a long lingering finish to this excellent Pinot Noir. Awarded 94 points by *Wine Spectator*; 700 cases were made.

2014 Clay Court Pinot Noir

Beautifully balanced; modern, clean, and serious yet purposely fashioned for earlier consumption. Showcases high-toned, tangy, spicy red fruits; minerals; baking spices; and a distinct violet note. Good bracing acidity sets up the long floral-accented finish. Drink in 5 to 7 years. Awarded 91 points by *Wine Spectator*; 700 cases were made.

2014 Mount Richmond Pinot Noir

This Pinot is bolder, darker, and more brooding, with a spectrum of spicy, sappy black forest fruits. The generous succulent palate is supple and sleek in the mouth; the fruit is ripe, juicy, and sweet, supported by big-boned, powerful tannins and high acidity. Drink in 5 to 8 years. Awarded 93 points by *Wine Spectator*; 1,200 cases were made.

2009 Five Mountain Pinot Noir

Upon opening, this bottle displayed a savory dark-fruited nose of *sous-bois*, cola, sweet vanilla pod, and ivy wrapped around a solid core of dark cherry, mulberry, and red and black plum flavors. This wine has put on weight as it's aged, and has a dense, spicy black-cherry feel. The tannins and acidity have integrated well and the palate shows a medium-long textured finish. Drink now. A total of 700 cases were made.

ELK COVE VINEYARDS

27751 NW Olson Road
Gaston, Oregon 97119
503.985.7760
info@elkcove.com
www.elkcove.com

SOKOL BLOSSER
Dayton

Bill Blosser and Susan Sokol graduated from Stanford in June 1966 and married soon after. Following the birth of their first child, in 1970, they drove their 1968 VW camper up to an abandoned prune orchard 30 miles southwest of Portland and planted their first cuttings. Bill and Susan soon joined the ranks of Oregon's earliest winemakers with their 1977 inaugural vintage. Two years later, their wines garnered recognition at the International Wine and Spirits Competition in London, where six Sokol Blosser entries won several golds.

In 2006, while celebrating their 30th harvest, Susan Sokol Blosser published her memoir, *At Home in the Vineyard*. Today, their children are in charge of the winery as co-presidents. Son Alex is the head winemaker and daughter Alison is the CEO.

Tasting Notes: Sokol Blosser

2014 Dundee Hills Chardonnay

A crisp, lithe wine exhibiting aromas of fresh white orchard fruits: lemon, peach, apple, and pear flavors float on a high-toned, medium-bodied frame. With time, notes of banana, white pepper spice, custard, vanilla cream, and an interesting saline note appear. This wine has a sinewy, mineral-infused finish. Drink now through 2018. A total of 700 cases were produced.

2011 Peach Tree Block Pinot Noir

An expressive wine with a spicy core of black cherry and secondary nuances of dried spices, vanilla, tobacco, chocolate, cola, and damp earth. It has great length of flavor. Drink in 5 to 9 years. Awarded 90 points by *Wine Spectator*; 200 cases were made.

2012 Estate Cuvée Pinot Noir

A beautiful wine that really demonstrates the quality of its terroir, exhibiting complex aromas of dark fruits, herbs and spices, beef blood, chocolate, vanilla, and *sous-bois*, plus an interesting gamey feral note. This cuvée has a good weight of fruit, spicy accents, and firm but sweet, tight-grained medium tannins; smooth and interesting with a savory note. Drink in 3 to 7 years. Awarded 92 points by *Wine Spectator*; 750 cases were made.

SOKOL BLOSSER

5000 NE Sokol Blosser Lane
Dayton, Oregon 97114
503.864.2282
info@sokolblosser.com
www.sokolblosser.com

Above: **Pinot Noir barrels at Elk Cove.**
Pages 260–261: **The vineyards at Sokol Blosser.**

Glossary

AVA

The initials AVA stand for American Viticultural Area. An AVA defines a designated wine grape-growing region within the United States and is validated by the Alcohol and Tobacco Tax and Trade Bureau (TTB) of the U.S. Department of the Treasury. Wineries and other petitioners request a defined AVA to establish their place in the wine world. In early 2015, there were 230 designated AVAs in the United States. Once an AVA is established, at least 85% of the grapes used to make a wine must be grown within that specified area for the bottle to be labeled as part of that AVA.

Acid

Acids are extracted from the fresh grapes and are intensified in the winery by the fermentation process. These acids are essential in the creation and makeup of balanced wines. Acidity enlivens the taste and bouquet and provides stuffing for further development, similar to the way that tannin creates structure. Without these two essential elements a wine becomes "flabby."

Aftertaste (or Finish)

The flavor that persists in the mouth after swallowing is an important factor in determining the quality of a wine, as the flavor of most well-made wines will linger in the mouth. The longer the aftertaste, the more it indicates a superbly made wine.

Alcoholic Fermentation

A biological process where yeast consumes the inherent sugars in the grape juice and converts those sugars into alcohol and carbon dioxide.

Astringency

A rough, coarse, unpleasant sensation in the mouth caused by excessive tannins and acidity, especially when a wine is young or at the end of its life. Extended bottle age will undoubtedly "smooth" out tannins, but a wine's acidity will never recede once bottled, thus old wines with faded tannins still can easily exude an astringent quality.

Austere

Severe tasting; typically of a young wine, tight with youthful tannins cloaking the submerged fruit. Age is the remedy, usually softening and opening up this angular description. Austerity with age is most commonly indicative of a loss of the wine's fruit while still retaining an overly tannic frame. However, on a bright note, it can also describe a desired "lean" style of winemaking that purposely showcases its delicate mineral and terroir attributes rather than a simple swath of monolithic fruits.

Wine barrel as garden decoration at Domaine Drouhin Oregon.

Balance

This term is used when all the components in winemaking supposedly merge—acidity, tannins, fruit, and alcohol—either harmonizing or, in some cases, not.

Barrel Aging

Once the fermentation of the juice is completed, the finished wine can mature and soften its overt tannins in a variety of different barrels, depending on the producer's desired style. New oak imparts a powerful, creamy taste; second-year barrels have a soft, vanilla edge, while inert barrels and stainless steel impart no influence at all. Where the barrels are made is also a factor: New American Oak creates strong-tasting and direct flavors of vanilla, as the wood grain is small. French Oak is also powerful, but more creamy and complex in final taste due to its larger grain. Elapsed time in barrel is also an important consideration in terms of taste; the more time spent in barrel, the more the wine will taste of oak.

Barrel Fermentation

A relatively new method where fermentation takes place in small oak barrels instead of the usual stainless steel. This gives the resultant wines a very dense, oaky taste.

Biodynamic Viticulture

An ancient yet recently revived method of grape growing that revolves around the awareness of planetary movements and its calculated effect on what we grow on our own planet. The aim is to create harmony in growth between all the natural elements the land offers, thus ensuring a better balance between its components. "Magnetic" forces among the moon, planets, and stars are carefully calculated and a mystical timetable of when to plant, pick, etc., is strictly adhered to. Bizarre pagan rituals, such as burying goat horns, are taken very seriously by some of the best wine producers all over the world. Chemicals in the vineyards are kept at a bare minimum, with winemakers choosing and promoting alternative natural defenses such as carefully introduced insects and other wildlife to keep natural pests at bay.

Body

The physical weight of the wine in the mouth, which can range from delicately light, as in the wines of Germany's Mosel Valley, to rich and thick, as in those found in the southern Rhône. Neither, of course, is "wrong"; it is just a matter of preference.

Bouquet

The smell of the wine.

Clone

A recognized strain of an individual grape that has been endowed or enhanced with certain attributes in a laboratory, usually for resistance to certain diseases.

Cold Fermentation

A method that utilizes slow, long fermentation temperatures in a closed tank to gently coax maximum freshness out of the grapes.

Cuvée

A bottle from a particular vat or selected barrel, derived from the French word *cuve*, meaning "vat." It could also be a wine made from a certain combination of grapes, such as champagne cuvées. When used with champagne, it also means the house's most prestigious wine.

Diurnal Temperatures

A meteorological term that relates to the variation of temperatures from the high of the days to the cool of the nights. These shifts are particular in terms of viticulture, with the variation ensuring good levels of acid and sugar and increasing the ripeness during the day, while the sudden drop at night preserves natural acids.

Filter

The separation of solids and liquids by filtration of the juice through a semipermeable membrane, leaving a fine liquid. In winemaking, filters can remove bacteria and yeast cells. Some winemakers use extensive filtration, some filter in moderation, and others don't use any.

Ice Wine

An intense, rare wine that's produced by letting the grapes freeze on the vines before and during the very late harvest. Upon reaching the winery the frozen grapes are pressed and the water, as ice, is easily separated from the intensely sweet fruit juice and discarded.

Lees

The sediment or junk that settles on the bottom of the tank after fermentation. It is a mixture of dead cells, tartrates, and organic matter. In some cases lees are desired, and wines (mostly white) can often be left "on the lees" for extended periods, to develop extra richness and flavor.

Must

The mixture of solids and juice produced after crushing the unfermented grapes in the winery.

Oaky

Term used to describe the woody or vanilla smells and flavors contributed to wine that is stored in oak barrels. Newer barrels provide a stronger impact. The longer the wine is left in the oak barrel, the more its flavor will be influenced. If the oak flavor dominates, the wine is termed over-oaked, meaning it is flawed.

Old World

In wine, this refers to the places where wine was first celebrated, particularly in the Mediterranean region. Old-world techniques refer to the ancient methods of winemaking, relying more on tradition and less on science. Wine producers are fond of saying they employ old-world techniques to indicate that their wines are at least partly made in traditional ways.

Oxidation

A process that occurs when grapes, juice, or wine has been exposed to air, which alters the wine. A small amount of oxidation can open up a wine and be beneficial to the taste. Too much can ruin it, turning the wine brown and giving it the taste of cheap port.

Phylloxera

An aggressive louse that attacks the roots of the vine and destroys the plant. In the late 1880s, phylloxera devastated the vineyards of Europe and eventually, large parts of the world. Winemakers have successfully curbed its influence by grafting American rootstocks, resistant to the bugs, onto the initial vine. It still remains a problem as the insects evolve and attack even the grafted stock.

Racking

A method of clarifying wine by siphoning off the sediment from a barrel of wine and pouring the wine into a clean barrel, thus leaving behind the murky lees.

Table Wine

A term used by winemakers around the world to describe wine that is moderate in alcohol. Most commonly, "table wines" refer to dry, still wines used for meals, as opposed to sweet wines or sparkling wines intended for dessert.

Tannin

A substance extracted from the grape's skin, seeds, and stems, which gives a necessary structured feel or framework to a wine while providing extended longevity in the bottle. The harshest of tannins are usually softened by initial oak aging in the winery, but some powerful extracted wines need even more softening, which comes in the form of bottle maturation.

Terroir

From the French *goût de terroir* or "taste of the earth," a combination of aspects that go into the entirety of the vineyard's climate, soil, and exposure to sun—and everything else that affects the grapes. Every vineyard is believed to have its own unique terroir, and so every wine reflects where it was planted. Many wines of today have become ubiquitous, and with the addition of new oak, have taken on a universal feel that makes it difficult to place their origin.

Ullage

The space at the top of the bottle when wine is lost by leakage or evaporation. If the space is significant, the wine can be spoiled due to the presence of too much oxygen in the bottle.

Unfiltered

Wine that has not been filtered for clarification. Some winemakers believe that filtering can strip the wine of flavor. Unfiltered wine can be less clear than its filtered counterparts.

Outside the tasting room at Ken Wright Cellars.

Vertical

As in a vertical flight, which is a tasting of wines from multiple years by the same producer, such as a 2010, 2012, and 2013 Eyrie Vineyards Original Vines Pinot Noir. The reason for a vertical tasting is to highlight the variations between vintages.

Vinification

Turning grapes into wine.

Vintage

The year the grapes were grown and harvested. The vintage year usually appears on the wine label, though some famous wines carry no vintage year because they are a combination of wine blends from various years. In the United States, law dictates that the vintage year on the bottle indicate that 95% of the grapes were harvested that year.

Vintner

The person who makes, and/or sells, the wine.

Viticulture

The science, management, and growing of vines and grapes in vineyards.

Yield

How much fruit a vineyard will produce over a given year. Yields are dependent on weather conditions, age of vines, their exposure to sun, planting density, and grape variety utilized. In general, high yields are associated with lower-quality wines while smaller yields denote higher-quality wines. However, the ratio of yield to quality is very complex.

Photography Credits

Adelsheim family archive: 12, 76, 77, 78, 79 (left), 80, 81, 84.

Archery Summit archive: 189, 190–191, 195, 196, 198, 200–201, 249.

Adam Bacher Photography: 41.

Beaux Frères archive: 18, 91, 92, 93, 94, 95, 97 (top), 98, 100, 101.

Alan Brandt: 169, 170–171.

Anna Campbell: 3, 232, 235, 244, 252, 256–257, 258, 259.

Campbell family archive: 255.

John D'Anna: 14–15, 20 (top), 180–181.

Kent Derek: 79 (right).

Erath Winery archive: 57, 65.

Evenstad family: 110.

Eyrie archival photos are Copyright © The Eyrie Vineyards: 25, 26, 28, 29, 30–31.

Charles Gullung: 19, 75, 82–83, 85, 87.

Hannah Hasbrook (shot on an iPhone): 114–115.

Andrea Johnson Photography: 47, 51 (bottom), 59, 70–71, 168, 178, 184, 185, 233, 234.

Richard Knapp: 197.

Moment of Thyme: 207, 210, 212.

Patricia Green Cellars archive: 209, 211 (bottom), 214–215, 217, 219.

Polara Studio: cover, 11 (top), 20 (bottom), 22–23, 43, 45, 48–49, 51 (top), 250–251.

Ponzi Vineyards archive: 16, 44, 50, 53.

Michael Richeson: 124.

RJ Photography: 135, 136, 138–139, 140, 141, 145, 267.

Linda Sunshine: 246.

Carolyn Wells-Kramer Photography: 6–7, 8, 13, 17, 42, 86, 107, 108, 111, 113, 117, 118, 167.

Julie Wise: 9, 10, 11 (bottom), 21, 27, 32, 33, 35, 36, 61, 62, 63, 64, 67, 96, 97 (bottom), 99, 112, 116, 125, 128, 129, 130, 144, 149, 150, 152, 153 (right), 157, 161, 162, 165, 172, 177, 179, 182, 192, 193, 194, 199, 202, 208, 211 (top), 213, 222, 223, 224–225, 226, 227, 228, 229, 230, 231, 245, 247, 253, 254, 260–261, 262, 270, 272.

Doreen Wynja, Eye of the Lady Photography, McMinnville: 153 (left).

Acknowledgments

No one could possibly write a book like this without the help of legions of folks who agreed to meet with us, to sit down and talk for hours, to supply us with stories, photos, research, and contacts, to answer our questions and to share their amazing wines and winemaking talents. We had some barrel tastings in Oregon that literally left us weak with gratitude. We are so enormously grateful to everyone who helped—from the winemakers to the hospitality managers, from the winery assistants to the PR people, and everyone in-between. We apologize for bugging you in our relentless pursuit of high-resolution photos and answers to our myriad of questions. We thank you for reviewing our text and fixing our mistakes.

One of the main reasons we fell in love with the Willamette Valley, aside from the Pinot Noir, was the people that we met. They sure like to do a lot of hugging in the great state of Oregon! We had some amazing conversations and we learned so much from all the generous souls who met with us, sometimes on very short notice.

Here, in alphabetical order, are the amazing Oregonians we want to thank:

David Adelsheim, Jim Anderson, Adam Bacher, Margaret Barry, Vanessa Bazzani, Josh Bergström, Jeb Bladine, Véronique Boss-Drouhin, Jillian Bradshaw, Shirley Brooks, Adam Campbell, Anna Campbell, Laurel Carroll, Linda Cline, Kira Cooper, John D'Anna, Steve Doerner, Michael Etzel, Mikey Etzel, Grace and Ken Evenstad, Tom Gerrie, Joseph Granados, Patricia Green, Vanessa Haddick, Ryan Harris, Will Hoppes, Gary Horner, Andrea Johnson, Kurt Johnson, Nate Klostermann, Richard Knapp, Taylor Knight, Jason Lett, Jack & Lynn Loacker, Elyse Lovenworth, Cathy Martin, Kayt Mather, Chris Mazepink, Ivory McLaughlin, Paul Mentzer, David Millman, Sashi Moorman, Cody Newell, Stephanie O'Bryant, Dave Paige, Rajat Parr, Ryan Pennington, Heather Perkin, Polara Studio, Luisa Ponzi, Caroline Schoonveld, Raechel Sims, Alex Sokol Blosser, Rollin Soles, Carly Sperling, Miranda Stafford, Corby Stonebraker-Soles, Diana Szymczak, Mark Tarlov, Sarrah Torres, Diane Victoria, Carolyn Wells-Kramer, Cody Wright, Ken Wright, Doreen Wynja, and Joleen Zanuzoski.

And a great big shout out of love and appreciation to our incredible publishing team: Lena Tabori, Katrina Fried, Gregory Wakabayashi, Ellen Leach, Natasha Tabori Fried, Clark Wakabayashi, David Barraclough, Miles Feinberg, and Bob Wise.

Nick Wise & Linda Sunshine

Biographies

Nick Wise was born in NYC in 1969 and moved with his family to the UK before he was two. He returned to the US for high school at the Peddie School in Hightstown, New Jersey. He went on to Tufts University in Boston, earning degrees in art and art history. After graduation he began writing books on popular culture, seven of which were completed and published, including books on Kurt Cobain and the Beach Boys. At the same time he'd always had a keen interest in wine and winemaking and earned a bachelors in wine at the Wine & Spirit Education Trust in London. During this time, he also worked for various historic English wine and spirit companies including John Armit and Fuller, Smith and Turner selling wine futures, mostly to the Far East. In 2003 he started a corporate champagne company called casevalue.com, which worked closely with companies such as LVMH, Bollinger, and many others in the champagne trade. The company was sold in 2011 so he returned to concentrate on his writing. He is the author of *Celebrity Vineyards* (Welcome Books, 2013) and co-author of *California Celebrity Vineyards* (Overlook-Omnibus, 2016). He currently lives in London and Los Angeles with his wife, Julie, and his Parson Jack Russell, Lily.

Linda Sunshine is the co-author of *California Celebrity Vineyards* (Overlook-Omnibus, 2016), and author of more than 50 books, including *How NOT to Turn Into Your Mother*, *She's Just THAT Into You*, *Women Who Date Too Much*, *All Things Alice*, *All Things Oz*, *The Family Dinner*, *The Family Dog*, *The Illustrated Woody Allen Reader*, and *The New York Times* best seller, *Plain Jane Works Out*. She has written extensively about Hollywood and the making of feature films. She lives in Los Angeles.

Julie Wise grew up in Beaune in Burgundy, France, and worked for ten years in French gastronomy and wine. She met her husband, Nick, in California, and today the couple share their time between two homes, in Venice Beach and in the heart of London. This project brings together her passion for photography and interest in enology and has joyfully introduced her to the incredible wines and wineries of Oregon.

Opposite: **The vineyards at Erath Winery.**

Above: **Nick Wise in the cellar at
Cristom Vineyards.**
Cover: **Photograph of Ponzi Vineyards
by Polara Studio.**
Page 2: **Map of Willamette Valley
by Gregory Wakabayashi.**